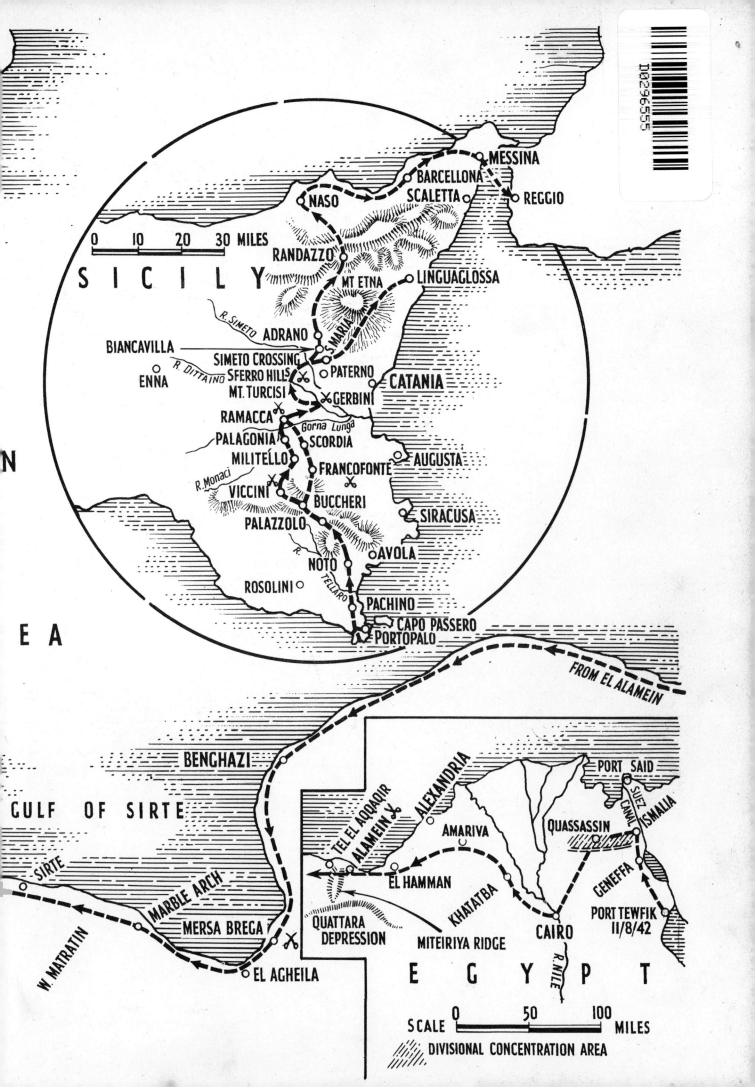

The 51st Highland Division at War

The 51st Highland Division at War

Roderick Grant

LONDON

IAN ALLAN LTD

The capture of Gennep. Troops of the Division move into the outskirts of the town, February 1945.

First published 1977.

ISBN 0 7110 0735 7.

Designed by Anthony Wirkus LSIA

© Roderick Grant, 1977

Published by Ian Allan Ltd, Shepperton, Surrey,
and printed in the United Kingdom by
Ian Allan Printing Ltd.

Crossing the Rhine by raft,
March 23, 1945.

Also by Roderick Grant:

Non-Fiction
Adventure In My Veins
Seek Out The Guilty
Where No Angels Dwell
Gorbals Doctor
The Lone Voyage of Betty Mouat

Fiction
The Dark Horizon (with Alexander Highlands)
The Stalking of Adrian Lawford
The Clutch of Caution

Contents

To the wives, mothers and children
of the men of the 51st Highland
Division, and to the three Battalions of
the 51st Highland Volunteers who,
today, bear the name made famous in
two World Wars.

Foreword

Major General Douglas Wimberley CB DSO MC DL LLD
General Officer Commanding HD 1941~1943

The author of '51st Highland Division at War' has not set out in any way to write an account, let alone a history, of the Division in World War II. What he has done is to collect several hundred good illustrations of the period, and to intersperse these with a number of graphic and interesting witnesses' accounts.

This combination will certainly bring back memories among all those who fought in the Division, and under the well-known Highland Division sign, and indeed their families also.

It is not for me, a member of that gallant company, to extol our prowess, but the reader has only to turn to the end of the book and note what the leaders of our country in both World Wars have said about us. While many of the various accounts quoted in this book themselves bear witness to our high morale and esprit on all of the long way from the Saar in 1940 to Bremen in 1945 except for a temporary lapse of some two months duration in Normandy, I notice that most of these accounts are provided, however, by members of the Highland Regiments. In a sense this is to be expected, because in an Infantry Division it is the battalions which, over all, undergo the most danger and suffer by far the most casualities. Let no young reader, however, imagine that in either great war it was only the Infantry that fought. Artillery, Engineers, Signals, Machine Gunners and all the Administrative Services were vital links in our successes. All were equally proud to be part of the Highland Divisional team.

Left: Major General Douglas Wimberley from a drawing by Ian Eadie.

Far left: Two Black Watch Sergeants:- Sgt D Stevenson of Kirkintilloch, Sgt A Dixon of Dunfermline.

Further, no infantryman in World War II is ever likely to forget the presence, or absence, of the Tanks allotted to us by higher commanders to help and support us in almost every battle, engagement or action.

Douglas Wimberley

Introduction

A verse appearing in the Scots Press regarding the 51st Highland Division in 1943

'Ye canna mak' a sojer wi' braid an' trappins braw
Nor gie him fightin' spirit when his back's agin the wa'
It's the breedin' in the callants that winna let them whine
The build o' generations frae lang, lang, syne'.

The 51st Highland Division, as a military formation, is a direct descendant of the Highland Regiment* which first went on parade at Aberfeldy among the hills of Perthshire in 1740. In the annals of military history the Scottish infantry regiments have earned a distinguished place for themselves because of their doggedness, courage and tenacity in, at times, the face of seemingly insurmountable odds.

In 1908 a reorganisation of the Territorial Army brought all of the kilted Highland regiments together to form the 51st Highland Division and by 1918, at the end of World War I, the Division, although only ten years old, had already established a legendary aura due to its performance in the major battle zones.

As legends are prone to do, the mystique of its prowess grew throughout the years until, shortly after the outbreak of World War 2 in 1939, it found itself in France as part of the British Expeditionary Force. Here, although commanded by an able general, Victor Fortune, the 51st Highland Division became enmeshed in questionable military and political manoeuvres by the French and British Governments. When called upon to do so it fought long and hard – and well, upholding its long tradition. Eventually, in June 1940, circumstances forced General Fortune to surrender at St Valery-en-Caux and the majority of this famed infantry Division of the British Army found themselves being marched off to prisoner-of-war camps.

*The Highland Regiment (The Black Watch).

Just over a year later a new 51st Highland Division was formed and in August 1942, with the 1st/7th Battalion The Middlesex Regiment as their machine-gun battalion, arrived to join the Eighth Army in the Western Desert. They were now under the command of Major-General Douglas Wimberley.

From then, until the end of the war, the 51st Highland Division was to take part in thirteen major battles: El Alamein, Medenine, Mareth, Akarit, Enfidaville, Tunis, landing in Sicily, Adrano (all 1942/43); Odon, Caen, Falaise, Rhineland, Rhine (1944/45).

By their action in these battles the Division gave birth to a new legend. As fighters their exploits and tactics became revered and their achievements were recognised to such an extent that they found themselves in the forefront of many major battles. Of the thirty infantry, armoured and airbone divisions which took part in officially listed battles during World War 2 the 51st Highland Division is listed as having taken part in more than any other division, with the exception of the 7th Armoured, the 'Desert Rats' and the 56th Division. Only six divisions took part in as many as ten battles; the average of the rest is five.

This book is not concerned with the strategy of these battles, nor indeed the tangled muddle that existed in France in 1940 which sent the original division into captivity. I have set out to show what life was like for those of all ranks in the 51st Highland Division during the years of World War 2. Eye-witness accounts of events both great and small, humorous, dramatic and commonplace incidents, are provided by former serving members.

Glory and honour there undoubtedly was, and it is here in both the narrative and the illustrations, many of which have never been published before. But before there can be glory and honour there must be a spirit of comradeship which is capable of tackling the mundane tasks as brilliantly as the more important ones.

This spirit was implated at all levels of rank in the 51st Highland Division and throughout this book it is the main element I have attempted to portray in providing what I hope will be an evocative picture of this famous Division at war.

In doing this I have been helped enormously by more people than I could possibly name. I wish to thank everyone who got in touch with me to provide information. Every detail, no matter how small, was important to me in my research. There are a number of people, however, who deserve a special mention if only for having kept calm and collected during months of correspondence and questioning from a determined author intent on coaxing from them every scrap of information they possessed.

They are: J. C. Adam, Charles Barker, George Blackhall, Alexander Brodie, James Fulton, Ian E. Kaye, Robert Kennedy, Hugh Macrae, Charles Shears, Douglas Thow and Douglas Wimberley.

Sincere thanks must go to Edward Hine of the Photographic Library, Imperial War Museum, who devoted much time to assisting me in my research for photographs and Barry Kitts of the Department of Art, Imperial War Museum, for helping me choose suitable paintings by war artists. Also to Bob Field for help in compiling and collating the photographs and caption material and to Chris Clemens for her usual good work in typing the manuscript.

Roderick Grant

To St Valery - and Surrender

Men of the Gordon Highlanders march to Aberdeen railway station on the first leg of their journey to France.

At the end of January, 1940, when the 51st Highland Division went ashore at Le Havre, Normandy was in the grip of a severe winter. There had been several weeks of intense frost. So great was the weight of ice on the trees that branches were constantly breaking under the strain and on the country lanes and farm tracks great ruts and potholes made travel both on foot and by vehicle extremely difficult. Within a couple of days a thaw started. It rained non-stop. A great mass of fog settled over the countryside. Through this trudged the troops, marching on what had become a carpet of mud. Then, almost overnight the frost returned. Even the men who had come from the most northerly parts of Scotland had never experienced cold so biting, so cutting as this. For the next month there was to be little respite as the battalions moved towards the Belgian frontier.

This then, was the 51st Highland Division's introduction to service with the British Expeditionary Force, before in April being moved to the Saar under French command, and the Franco-German border. There then followed periods spent in the defence of several important lines and positions and patrols whose purpose was to hamper and observe the enemy and provoke him to fight. The Germans were stalked with grenades and light machine-guns in the manner described in an official report prepared by Second Lieutenant A. L. Orr Ewing of the 7th Argyll and Sutherland Highlanders:

"I left our own wire near F.9 in the Grossenwald at 2300 hours and made my way to the south-east corner of the Lohwald. I lay up in the trees on the right-hand side. About 0130 hours I heard someone moving in the wood and ten minutes later more movement. I lay quiet for five minutes and then decided to investigate. I left four men with two automatic guns in the trees to cover me and also to shoot anyone trying to leave the corner of the wood. With the remaining men I moved forward between the stream and the wood.

About forty yards away from me I saw three men running from the wood towards the stream. I opened fire with my sub-machine gun and two men dropped. Heavy firing from at least four tommy guns immediately opened on my flank. My patrol and I all dropped flat and continued to fire and throw grenades. About eight or ten men then left the wood and opened fire. More men in the wood also fired on us. One man advanced towards us, but was severely hit in the stomach. At least two more were hit by grenades, as we

12

Throughout the months of April and May,
1940 the Division's role to give support to
the French forces was one that was
fraught with difficulties. Many of the
military decisions taken by the French
both alarmed and dismayed the British
and there were times when withdrawal to
a fresh position was favoured by the
British but opposed by the French and
other occasions when the French decision
to pull back, without fully consulting the
British, left the supporting forces even
more vulnerable to hostile attack.

On the matter of military strategy and
tactics it is an episode of history that can
still arouse fierce controversy, but
whatever the rights and wrongs it is clear
that when the greater part of the Division
was pulled back to the vicinity of St
Valery-en-Caux near Dieppe, with a view
to its evacuation across the Channel, such
was the muddle in communications
between the French, the Government in
London and the forces in the field that a
situation of almost total chaos was only
prevented by strict military discipline
being observed by individual commanders.

On the morning of June 11, 1940 Major-
General Victor Fortune who, as Commanding Officer of the Division, had the

heard them screaming. The enemy threw
stick-grenades, one landing near my
batman and me, cutting us both and temporarily blinding me with blood.

Owing to the superior numbers of the
enemy and the fact that our ammunition
was running low, we withdrew about sixty
yards under covering fire from the four
men we had left in our rear. The enemy
then also withdrew and we heard them
talking on the other side of the stream. As
it was then our time to return, we made
our way back to our own wire.''

The early months in France were spent in a desperate attempt to improve the defences along the Belgian border which was not covered by the Maginot Line complex. In this picture a working party of the 1st Bn, The Gordon Highlanders, returns after a morning's digging at Templeux.

unenviable task of trying to satisfy the requirements of the French while, at the same time, seeing to it that his own soldiers were not endangered without justification, issued a directive to his commanding officers.

"The Navy will probably make an effort to take us off by boat, perhaps in two nights. I wish all ranks to realise that this can only be achieved by the full co-operation of everyone. Men may have to walk five or six miles. The utmost discipline must prevail.

"Men will board the boats with equipment and carrying arms. Vehicles will be rendered useless without giving away what is being done. Carriers should be retained as the final rearguard. Routes back to the nearest highway should be reconnoitred and officers detailed as guides. Finally, if the enemy should attack before the whole force is evacuated, all ranks must realise that it is up to them to defeat them. He may attack with tanks, and we have quite a number of anti-tanks behind. If the infantry can stop the enemy's infantry, that is all that is required, while anti-tank guns and rifles inflict casualties on armoured fighting vehicles."

What was developing was a race against time, but the Germans were pressing home their advantage with great skill and speed. Almost as the 51st were moving into St Valery the enemy were closing in around the town. So great was their superiority in the area that when a number of naval vessels of differing sizes approached St Valery to effect an evacuation they were either driven back by heavy fire or sunk. The sloop *Hebe II*

managed to take off about 80 men from a beach close to the town but was holed by shell-fire and sank. Then fog came down, followed by heavy rain and visibility was such that those on land could see nothing of the ships and those on the vessels had no clear view of the shore.

Douglas Thow was in the Gordon Highlanders still trying to break through the encircling Germans so that St Valery could be reached.

"Those last two days were the worst. We were under attack almost constantly and at times it was difficult to tell friend from foe. The night of the 11th we were still overjoyed at the prospect of being taken off. All the heavy equipment was destroyed to prevent it from falling into German hands. I remember the fog and that last night when, I think, the order 'every man for himself' was issued. Events were confused, but suddenly the shelling stopped and we were told to lay down our arms. The Germans had surrounded us completely. That was the end. There was no panic. Some men tried to escape and I am sure some succeeded. Our mood was very low and I shall always remember seeing men crying there."

Luck was on the side of Lt Col. J. C. Adam, commanding officer of 154 (Highland) Field Ambulance Unit.

"During the withdrawal from the River Bresle the troops were dead-beat and if a convoy was held up for any reason the drivers promptly went to sleep, and had to be roused to restart. On June 9, 1940 'Ark Force' was formed. It consisted of the remnants of 154 Brigade and included 154 Fd Amb. The intention was that it would

form the perimeter force at Le Havre and the Division would follow.

"We ran into very black cloud – which turned out to be smoke from the burning oil tanks at Le Havre. It was impossible to see the road and my driver sat on the bonnet of the car and said "Right or Left-hand down" as we crawled along. We passed through St Valery-en Caux, by which time we had passed through the blanket of smoke, about 0600 hrs on June 10th. Later that day we took the coast road to Fécamp and Etretat and on to Le Havre. Later we learned that Rommel was on the main road on his way to cut off the Division at St Valery. It was a very lucky escape for us."

Robert Kennedy, who was a private in the 1st Battalion, The Gordon Highlanders, has a lasting memory of the large number of vehicles abandoned and demobilised in the countryside around St Valery.

"As we drove into St Valery there were all sorts of vehicles, lorries and jeeps, a tremendous number, machine-gunned and burned out. They were everywhere – just left derelict. On our last night in the town we were shelled, bombed and machine-gunned. We replied as best we could, but we were vastly outnumbered.

"When we were captured there were only about a dozen of us together at the time. Somehow, I thought we were the only ones being taken prisoner. But after we were searched and marched out of St Valery up the hill to a field overlooking the sea, I was amazed by the hundreds of men gathered together under guard in that field. On arriving there I saw General Fortune, our Divisional Commander, being spoken to by Rommel, the German

General. I realised then that it was all over for us. It was a sad day."

For Private J. McCready of the 1st Black Watch the escape from enemy-held territory to Brigade Headquarters was made all the more hazardous and difficult by the great numbers of French troops and refugees choking the roads.

"Occasionally we passed piles of them dead at the roadside, having been machine-gunned from the air or just rolled aside by tanks. How we ever got out of that was a miracle. We never got back to the Battalion after that. We were stuck in an orchard near Brigade and we just simply waited for things to happen. Mr Telfer-Smollet went off to reconnoitre new positions about mid-day, and never returned.

"By this time we were being shelled, machine-gunned, and I think all the weapons that could be used were against us. This continued until after dark and I am afraid I fell asleep at the roadside. Mr Allison gave out all the cigarettes he had and we just simply lay there. At two o'clock in the morning (June 12) I was told it was a case of every man for himself, so we all got bundled into the remaining five trucks and I must say I was completely unaware of what direction the coast lay in, or what was to be done. In fact, I was beyond caring about anything.

"Well, we moved off. I was in the back of the eight cwt with somebody sitting on my head. We had only gone half a mile when we were ambushed, by machine-gun. I scrambled out somehow and dived into the ditch, then the enemy started using Very lights and picked the men off with tommy-guns as they jumped off the

Battledress was introduced only gradually in the early months of the war, many of the Gordon Highlanders shown in this picture taken in April 1940 still retain their World War I-style tunics and are wearing kilts.

truck. I owe my life to the fact that I was in the last truck. I managed to scramble out of the ditch and along the bank. I almost got a burst into my back. They were using tracer and they almost burnt my ears with the heat. I came on a party of RE's at the roadside and they immediately scattered into the fields. I saw Mr Allison there. He was all right. He followed some RE's who went off to the right.

"I waited a few minutes and then made off after the ones who went to the left. We were spotted in the light and murderous fire broke out again. I don't know how far I crawled on my stomach, it seemed hours before that gunner got fed up, so with his last burst we gave him a volley from our rifles and it evidently disposed of him as the going was comparatively easy for a bit, until we ran into an enemy motor-convoy on the road. It was stopped, and I thought it was French. They must have got a surprise because we were well away when they opened fire on us. I don't think they hit anybody as it was fairly misty and that, coupled with darkness, helped us. After that it was fairly easy to the cliffs."

His Majesty, King George VI and French Chief of Staff, General Gamelin, take a ride on the underground railway which ran through the forts on the Maginot Line.

East of St Valery the coastline consists of cliffs, three hundred feet high, stretching unbroken to the small port Veules-les-Roses four miles away. It was to here that the Navy went on the night of June 11 when it became obvious that they would never be able to evacuate the troops from St Valery itself. They landed beach parties and the rescue got underway which resulted in 1350 British and 930 French soldiers being taken off. For many the way to the beach was down ropes slung against the face of the cliffs. One soldier who made such a descent was Private McCready.

"Someone started making a rope of rifle slings and I joined in. By the time we had it made it was daylight and the enemy were shelling from both sides. I was fourth man on the rope and it was two-and-a-half hours before I got down. The first man to go met his death as the slings snapped, but it was either chance it or get caught so over I went. What a drop; and bullets spattering all over. We were being machine-gunned and sniped all the time. However, I got down without mishap and struggled along two miles of beach to the boats.

"What a lot of dead men there were on that beach – it was littered with them. I had just got into the small boat when the bombers came. One boat was sunk with about thirty men in it. Only one man was saved. The ships put up a terrific barrage and brought down two planes. How I got on the ship is still a bit of a dream to me, but get on I did, and soaked to the skin and simply covered with mud. I just sprawled out on deck, out for the count. I soon got a rude awakening. The enemy started shelling from the cliff tops, but the

destroyers put paid to their career. All those who had rifles had to get up on the top deck and fire at the planes. So I fired my remaining bandolier.

"We lay there until it was decided that no more men could possibly be on the beach or on the cliffs."

At 1000 hours General Fortune decided to surrender. Several hours previous to this he had received orders to destroy all rifles, guns, ammunition and equipment. He had already set this in motion. It was a hard, difficult decision to take, perhaps the most controversial decision any general is called upon to make when in the forefront of battle. General Fortune was a highly respected general and in the particular circumstances his decision to call a halt to the fighting was a brave one. His men had been pressed beyond the limits of endurance, travelling long distances without proper rest and food. They had been under constant bombardment for weeks. Above all, supplies of available ammunition were all but exhausted. What did remain was of no consequence against the weight of the German armament. The 51st Highland Division, with the exception of 154 Brigade who had managed to push through to Le Havre and be taken off from there, prepared itself for the prisoner-of-war camps.

All the same, until the end, it had remained a cohesive division with discipline ruling supreme. It had displayed aggression in attack and stubbornness in defence. But against the impressive strength of the German forces and enmeshed in the unpredictable manoeuvring of the French Army this had not been enough to see them through. For the Scottish officers, non-commissioned officers and private soldiers, and the many Englishmen who enlarged the strength of the Division, it was hard to accept that they had been defeated. But their surrender meant an end to needless and mindless slaughter and for seeing this and accepting it as reality General Fortune deserves a special place of honour among the men who have commanded this battle-scarred and illustrious Division.

Writing in 1942 Eric Linklater said:
"The Division was a division till the end. It had no luck – the dice were loaded outrageously against it – and so it failed to maintain the legend that its predecessor had made in the first German war, for a legend needs a little luck to help it grow. But the Fifty-First had the other virtues of the old Division and the proof is this – that would prove the virtue of any division – that in spite of its accumulated weariness, the frustration of all its hope, the failure on its flank and its grievous losses, its spirit was unbroken. It suffered many casualties, but not the fatal one. Its hard core was fighting to the end, and discipline was last in the field."

Coming events cast their shadows . . . The Camerons stage a concert party in April 1940 before the German attack.

Surprise, speed and fire-power were the prime ingredients of the German Blitzkrieg. In 1940 the Wehrmacht seemed to be fighting a different war from the British and French.

Into Battle

Lieutenant Hugh Macrae (4th Bn, Seaforth Highlanders) recalls:

Whatever people may forget about their life during wartime those who have taken part in battles have the impressions of their experience imprinted indelibly on their minds. They remain permanently fixed in the subconscious because, for the soldier, there can be no greater test of endurance. The order of battle and the military objectives may have been prepared with absolute precision, but it is the execution of the plans that is paramount when the battle commences. For their success they are dependent on the skill, courage, initiative and determination of the men out there on the battlefield; ordinary men, who, within the space of a few minutes, may know fear, display great courage, behave with remarkable shrewdness and cunning, act in a foolhardy or foolish manner, sometimes without realising it at the time, showing every aspect of their character as the swiftly-moving events sweep them on towards their objective.

Many men have said that they never experienced greater loneliness than those moments in battle when, despite the close proximity of their comrades, the noise of exploding shells, the crackling, sweeping fire of machine-guns and the rumbling of tanks and armoured vehicles, caused such an impression of apparent confusion that they became certain the enemy fire was being directed against them personally. In that instant it became their own personal battle – for survival.

At the height of a battle there was little time for the individual to think about what might happen to him. That came afterwards when, during a period of calm, often a lull before the next onslaught, he could reflect and for the most part, be amazed just how lucky he had been to survive.

Hugh Macrae joined the 4th Battalion, Seaforth Highlanders in 1938 when the strength of the Territorial Army was doubled. Because of seven years previous service with another auxiliary unit he was commissioned directly into the Battalion as a lieutenant, to become, at the age of thirty-eight, the intelligence officer working with a staff of one sergeant, one corporal and six other ranks.

In June 1940, a few days before the capitulation at St Valery he went into battle ("my first real battle") was wounded and, later, evacuated from St Nazaire.

"We were all lined up for a dawn attack – along a start line. There were heavy tanks in front, light tanks next, with the infantry working closely with them. We started off at zero hour and for the first mile or so everything went fine. We met no opposition.

Then, suddenly, we ran into it. We were advancing up a gentle slope, over bare fields which were topped by a line of well-spaced trees which had the raised earth of the field boundaries running along between them. Immediately we reached this spot German machine and anti-tank guns opened up on us. The enemy had this line very well covered by their fire.

At once the infantry men threw themselves flat on the ground, as they were trained to do, but the firing continued for some considerable time. At least it seemed like an age to me. Personally, I could hear, and in some strange way could almost feel, the bullets passing extremely close to my head. A strange thought was that a miracle would happen so that the earth might open up and let me down into it. Twelve inches would have been sufficient to have given me complete cover.

However, the feeling passed and although a few men and one or two tanks were hit the advance continued. The tanks went forward and we followed. The Germans kept up their fire. About half-a-mile further on the heavy tanks ran into a minefield. Several were blown up almost at once and caught fire. As clouds of thick, dark smoke began to swirl around our heads there were further explosions as more mines were detonated. Both light and heavy tanks were being put out of action, the force of the explosions lifting them into the air, toppling many right over on to their sides. Amid the smoke there were tongues of flame and the shouts of the men still trapped inside their vehicles.

The Germans were now using

additional anti-tank guns and at least three machine-guns were concentrating their fire on us, sweeping the bare slopes, one to our right front, one to our left and another to our right rear. Our men were being hit at an alarming rate and such was the concentration of fire against us, together with the devastation being caused by the mines to our tanks, that the advance appeared to have come to a complete standstill.

I saw a heavy tank standing stationary some distance away. It was not on fire, but there was no sign of the crew. It occurred to me that I could make good use of this tank as cover from the machine-gun bullets, but on running across I found that no matter which side I went to, bullets were either striking the ground very close to me or hitting the tank and ricochetting off the metal sides.

I had just come round the rear when something hit me in one of my legs, knocking me down. Surprisingly, I felt little pain. As I sat on the ground I saw bullet strikes sending up dust to my left front and also swinging right towards me at about twelve to fifteen inch spacing. It was obvious that if I stayed where I was, within a couple of seconds I would be hit low down in the abdomen. I raised myself on my hands and feet, praying that the gunner would not get me in the wrists. Bullets were thudding into the ground all around me, in front of my face and on either side and just as I thought I had escaped that particular burst I felt one bullet graze my ankle. In that instant I noticed a shell hole only a few yards away. Although blood was seeping from my wounds my ankle did not appear to be broken. As fast as I could manage I shuffled and crawled towards the hole and dropped into it.

An immense feeling of relief came over me. For the moment, at least, I knew I was safe. It's also worth remembering that all this action happened in less time than it takes to tell; in close battle one's senses are extremely acute and quick. Reaction to them is instantaneous.

Now that I felt safe I took out my field dressing and bound up my wounds, noting with satisfaction that the blood soon coagulated and that I could move both my leg and ankle. Later, in the middle of the morning, Stuka dive bombers came over and bombed our positions; it was then that I realised this could well be the start of a German counter-attack. If they came on now I would probably end up as a wounded prisoner and I started to think of ways and means to avoid this fate.

I lay in the shell hole all day and under cover of darkness collected some men who could walk and got back to the Regimental Aid Post. The German counter-attack did not develop until the following morning by which time I was on my way to the Base hospital at Rouen.

When I look back on that day and try to recollect the thoughts that were passing through my head it seems that in such moments of stress one does not really have thoughts, merely reactions. Everything concerning an individual in battle is immediate, both in time and space and one's mind reacts instantaneously.

A good example of this occurred when I saw the strike of the bullets coming towards me as I sat on the ground. I immediately raised by body so that they would pass under me, which they did. Again, as I lay in the shell hole and had visions of being a wounded prisoner there were no thoughts of camps enclosed by barbed wire, or of being transported to them, or of German guards and poor rations and accommodation. My thoughts were, purely and simply, revolving around the sight of the men in field grey opposite us and how to avoid falling into their hands.

Later on, when on home service the wisdom of all the military training became brilliantly clear; the teaching of officers and men to react to a wide variety of circumstances quickly and, above all, correctly. I did my best to instal this into the men in my command and returned to Northern Europe in 1944 perfectly confident that everything would go well with us and with no fears for the future".

21

Impressions of an Infantryman-
(France 1939-40)

One that got away. A lorry
driver of the 51st Highland
Division who escaped from St
Valéry-en-Caux with his lorry
and a load of French refugees.

At the start of the war the territorial battalions were composed entirely of volunteers, strengthened with key men from their associated regular units. In certain cases as many as the Commanding Officer, his second-in-command and some Company Commanders would be ex-regulars while the adjutant, quartermaster, regimental quartermaster sergeant, regimental sergeant major and all the company sergeant majors were from the associated county regiment. The junior officers, NCO's and men were recruited from a comparatively small locality and at platoon level knew each other well.

This meant that from the start a high degree of unity was achieved and the resulting *espirit de corps* was judged to be an excellent example of how a tradition, evolved over centuries, could still work in modern times. In this account an officer in one of the territorial battalions vividly describes his thoughts and feelings as they set off for France – and subsequent disaster.

"After mobilisation a complete and thorough checking-out process began – sorting out unfits, over and under-age personnel – and the unit was soon moved to the Aldershot area where serious training commenced in earnest. Specialist courses were run for officers and NCO's and they returned to instruct their men, this along with all the normal infantry work.

The entire district around Aldershot was saturated with regular army units which included the Brigade of Guards depot at Pirbright. As a result the men began to emulate what was best in the regulars; drill, saluting, dress, turn out, the outward manifestations as well as the basic ones, good discipline, shooting, field craft and tactics improved tremendously. By Christmas, 1939, the Division was deemed fit to proceed overseas and after a spell of leave over the festive season embarkation commenced.

January and February in Northern France were months of severe cold and as the ground was frozen hard little could be done by way of training or work. However, as the weather improved we were moved up to the Belgian frontier and set to work on the defences. These appeared to be grossly inadequate and nobody appeared to be too concerned. There seemed to be no great urgency to get things done. A general easy-going spirit pervaded the whole country and when French soldiers or civilians were asked if the Germans would invade France this time, the answer was always *'Jamais, jamais.'* To

their great alarm and despondency they were soon to find out just how wrong their predictions had been.

The troops were billeted in villages and small towns and relations with the local people were very good. The rate of exchange with the franc was also in our favour and everyone found that things were cheap. The food in the cafes was also much to our taste.

Around this time in, what officialdom called, the interests of security the HD shoulder flash was withdrawn and a St Andrew's Cross in three different colours substituted. Each colour indicated a particular brigade and one, two or three bars in the same colour below the cross designated the battalions in the brigade. Cap badges were also withdrawn from the men, but officers and sergeants retained theirs. This was extremely bad for morale and could not have possibly confused the Germans or their informers, especially when pipe bands turned out to play in towns and villages with the battalion name, number and battle honours emblazoned on the drums.

April came and the weather was much improved when the order was given to move down to the Saar. This was welcomed by the troops who were by now finding life around Bailleul and Armentieres starting to become monotonous. We concentrated in Metz and during the night marched out to our positions.

In front of the Maginot proper were three infantry lines. These varied a little from place to place, but in our sector there was the *Ligne d'Arret* or stopping line just in front of the permanent forts. Some three miles in front of this was a continuous line of infantry trenches called the *Ligne de Recueil* or gathering line. Beyond this and a further three miles or so forward, right on the German border, was the *Ligne de Contact.* This was a line of platoon or company posts, not continuous but at a little distance from each other. The Germans had similar posts just within their border.

The original idea was that the Division would occupy their sector for six weeks, each brigade holding one-third of the front and each battalion doing two spells of one week each in each line.

At first all the action was in the *Ligne de Contact,* consisting of patrolling into Germany, raiding enemy posts and defending our own posts against similar activity. Action seldom penetrated as far as the *Ligne de Recueil* although constant vigilance had to be maintained here. The *Ligne d'Arret* was more peaceful and here

we could enjoy a rest with the troops having ample time to study the Maginot forts from the outside. All were very impressed by what they saw; the concealed artillery and machine-gun positions, observation posts and substantial anti-tank obstacles, all in some depth, gave a feeling of confidence. The civilian population between the border and the permanent forts had all been evacuated which gave us a freedom of action denied us in the north.

Our first take-over was from the 1st Battalion of the 11th Regiment of the French Foreign Legion. We looked forward to this as in pre-war days most people had read novels or seen films in which the Legion was the theme and its personnel the heroes of the occasion. Glamorous tales were spun of their prowess in love and war and due to the cinema screen the public had come to see them as smart, clean-cut figures in blue coats and kepis stalking adventure and romance.

We failed to notice any such features when we arrived. Instead, we saw a disunited collection of unshaven, ill-clad, dirty-looking individuals. On closer inspection we found that things were even worse than they had appeard at first sight. The state of sanitation was dreadful. Only dry lavatories were available in this rural countryside and no attempt had been made to empty them or in any way maintain some standard of hygiene. For sleeping they had straw to lie on, exactly

as we had, with six inch boards holding it in all round about six feet from the walls. Obviously, when clean straw had been issued they hadn't bothered to clean out the old, but simply had thrown the fresh stuff on top. As a result of this having gone on for so long the lower layers resembled manure. Finally, when they marched away their discipline was non-existent. In fact there was no attempt made to keep proper marching discipline. They looked and acted like a disorderly rabble.

This state of affairs could not be tolerated and everyone was detailed to start cleaning up the place. New latrines were dug and the dirty straw taken out and burned. From this, burning bombs exploded, bullets flew past our ears and it became obvious that whenever the Legionnaires had dropped anything – bullets, grenades – they had not bothered to pick it up.

In this part of the country both soldiers and civilians frequently wore brass badges in their buttonholes depicting a Maginot fort with the words *'Ils ne passerant pas'* underneath – the old Verdun battlecry. There is no doubt this was intended to be a morale booster, but it seemed to engender an attitude of slackness and a lack of urgency, much as we had seen in the north. Nevertheless, we considered that the Maginot proper was a strong line which would take a considerable effort to breach. Despite what its critics – many of whom never saw the line – said afterwards

The saddest picture in the history of the Division – the surrender at St Valéry-en-Caux. General Erwen Von Rommel photographed standing beside Major General Victor Fortune and other British officers, June 12, 1940.

I am certain that if it had been extended right along the border to the sea the course of the war would have been quite different. In actual fact, despite events, it never was breached.

On May 10, 1940, the entire Division was in front of the Maginot and we were surprised when, after 'stand-down', about five o'clock on a bright morning, whole flotillas of German aircraft could be seen flying eastwards. They were going home after the first bombing raids on the lines of communication behind us. They flew quite low, national markings being easily distinguished. Some French anti-aircraft guns opened up on them, but they went on unharmed. The Division had no anti-aircraft guns, the lack of which was to be felt later with great effect.

Around this time ground activity greatly increased. German patrols were larger and more aggressive. In some cases heavy artillery concentrations followed by large and determined infantry attacks took place. These were mostly beaten off, although some section and platoon posts were isolated by fire and the men killed or taken prisoner. Despite such losses, however, there was a tremendous spirit of adventure among the young fellows of the Division and this was sufficient to eliminate any feelings of depression which the setbacks might have engendered. In that closely wooded country, threaded by numerous streams and rivers, tanks or armoured vehicles were not used and the cover was so good that aircraft did little

damage. Individual skill and field craft were the order of the day and the practice of them in such terrain was not unpleasant.

We never completed our full six weeks in Lorraine. On May 20 we were withdrawn and placed in reserve to a French Division. Heavy attacks were being made at Montmedy, the extreme northern limit of the Maginot and it was said that we were being sent to halt them. In fact some units and headquarters staff actually left for that place. This move, however, was cancelled and we were ordered up to the northern front in Normandy. The order to entrain came to our battalion at 1400 hrs on a fine sunny afternoon and by 1410 hrs the leading company was marching down the road. There was an evident air of real professionalism in the air and at last we felt we were getting somewhere and doing something positive.

This was reflected throughout the entire Division. Troop trains were ordered, embarkation points established, straw for bedding commandeered and feeding points were laid on for the marching troops. All the transport, artillery, Bren carriers, cooks, water carts, the ammunition column and so on went by road, all marshalled according to their unit and purpose along predetermined routes. Advance parties were detailed to act as guides and to arrange rest and feeding points as well as to replenish the vast quantities of petrol being used; all this in a country being torn apart by war, over roads congested by refugees and subject to aerial bombardment several times a day. The move was accomplished in three days with practically no losses. The average soldier did his part well, but the staff work was superlative, as good as any army could muster and better than most.

The rail parties took a long route from Etain, by Vitry Le Francois, Orleans, Blois, Tours and Le Mans to Rouen, then by relays of French buses along Route National 28 to a crossroads in the middle of the Haute Foret d'Eu near the River Bresle. Here we met up with our transport which had miraculously arrived at the same point at the same time.

Mercifully, it had been a day of low cloud and dripping rain so that the German aircraft had been unable to operate and we suffered no casualties. On the other hand we were all soaking wet and in late evening when the order came to cross the river and advance along the Route National we welcomed it. The open country was better than the soaking forest and when the rain stopped the heat of our bodies dried our clothes. German advance units had penetrated as far as the Bresle, but on the previous day De Gaulle's Armoured Division had pushed them back a few miles. As a result we were able to occupy the villages of Le Transloy and Biencourt without opposition.

Whatever had been the original intention of sending our Division to this part of France, it was guessed that it was to open a way to the beleaguered army around Dunkirk. If this had been so, it was far too late. Dunkirk was surrounded and the evacuation was already gathering momentum. German units, in strength, had reached the Somme and there was heavy fighting around St Quentin and Cambrai. On its lower reaches the Somme had been crossed and two bridgeheads established; a small one at its mouth at St Valery-sur-Somme (not to be confused with St Valery-en-Caux) and a much larger one centred on the Abbeville bridges. Its base extended some four or five miles on either side of this town and its apex down Route National 28 for about six miles to the village of St Maxent.

The immediate tactical move now was to reduce this bridgehead and establish a firm line along the Somme. The Germans had occupied this ground for about fourteen days and although their outposts may have been lightly held their main defences were well prepared. Machine guns, field artillery, anti-tank guns and mines were positively sited and dug in.

On May 29 a joint attack was made on this by the 1st British Armoured Division and a French one. We followed closely, mopping up and taking some prisoners. The attack was only partially successful, but our 152 Seaforth and Cameron Brigade was able to advance about four miles and occupy the villages of Huchenneville, Behen, Bienfay and Moyenneville. The bridgehead still held, however, and we were dismayed to see a considerable number of British light tanks lying around wrecked and burned out. The following day a further attack was made, but on our flank it was unsuccessful and our infantry were unable to advance. However, on the left good progress was made on 153 Brigade's front and a point within two miles of the Somme was reached.

It was now decided to stage a full-scale attack on the remaining parts of the bridgehead to take place at dawn on June 4. Hasty preparations were made, additional artillery was brought up and all the tanks of the 31st French Division were mustered. The British 1st Armoured Division had retired to Rouen to refit.

Our particular task was to attack the German positions on the high ground overlooking the Somme, using Route National 28 as our right boundary and Mesnil Trois Foetus and Vaux farm as our left, a front of around 1500 yards.

Just beyond the starting line and in the centre of the 4th Seaforths' sector there was a wood called the Bois de Villers. This was secured by two companies of the 2nd Seaforths, but it necessitated putting two companies of the 4th on the right of the wood and two on the left. On the right of Route National 28 the 4th Camerons put in a simultaneous attack while on our left the 31st French Division did likewise.

Zero hour was 0300 hrs and at Zero minus 10 the artillery bombardment commenced. At 0330 hrs the French heavy tanks moved off from the starting line followed 15 minutes later by light tanks or Chenillettes as they called them. The 4th Seaforths B Company on the right and C Company on the left followed the light tanks closely and behind them, with a further gap of 15 minutes, came the remaining companies, D and A.

This programme was adhered to on the right, but on the left tanks were late in arriving. This meant that the infantry had to go on without them which resulted in a bad break in co-ordination.

For the first mile or so things went quite well, but then heavy machine gun and anti-tank fire was encountered. The German guns were well dug in and extremely well sited. They swept the bare slopes of the empty fields from different angles and there was no cover for our men. The anti-tank guns were similarly placed and mine fields had been laid in all the most likely places. The tanks ran into them and were brought to a halt, many of them catching fire while the infantry were mown down by the machine guns. In the centre the attack was brought to a halt before it reached the first objective but better progress was made on the flanks. Overall, however, the attack was a failure and it appears that the Germans had also made preparations to attack that same day. By the following morning they pressed it onwards with great ferocity.

It was apparent that the Division could not hope to hold its twenty mile front and so began the long rearguard action which ended so disastrously at St Valery-en-Caux. June 4 was also a disastrous day for the 4th Seaforths and 4th Camerons. Between them they lost 20 officers and 543 other ranks.

With the benefit of hindsight and years of further training since 1940 it is possible to see that there were several causes of failure. There was a distinct lack of proper reconnaissance – the Bois de Villers was not held by the enemy and could have been used as an excellent covered way to get the assault infantry at least half-a-mile further forward. The artillery support was quite inadequate and what there was of it was too often inaccurate. In fact, it did little but alert the Germans that something was coming. Minefields were undetected and the French tanks ran straight into them while the Chenillettes were not proof against the enemy anti-tank guns. There was also no method of communication between the French tanks and the Scottish infantry. It was as if two separate forces were fighting the same battle in the same fields with only the most vague idea of each other's intention. Finally, the young soldiers were apt to confuse commonsense with cowardice. They thought it was cowardly not to go forward against machine guns when, in fact, the sensible thing to have done was to first destroy the enemy positions with mortar or tank fire and so live to fight another day.

Looking back on history one must ask – if supposing this battle had been entirely successful would it have made any difference to the course of the war? The answer must be 'No'. For a variety of reasons France was beaten before she started and in the particular circumstances what was happening on her behalf was no more than a futile, although determined, effort.

The German attack on June 5 opened up all along the Divisional front, being particularly heavy against 154 Brigade on the seaward side. On this day the 7th Argylls put up a desperate fight at Franleau and suffered heavy casualties. On other parts of the front stout resistance was achieved by the 8th Argylls, 5th Gordons, 4th Camerons and many others.

There is one point I would like to make, however, which does not seem sufficiently stressed – that is, the actual fighting strength of the Division and the state it was in at St Valery. In this connection it should be borne in mind that the actual fighting strength of a Division is a good deal less than the total number of men in it. Heavy losses were suffered by the Gordons at the Saar and on June 5 the 4th Seaforths and 4th Camerons in the attack on Abbeville, the 7th Argylls at Franleau and their 8th Battalion the following day. These were all front line infantrymen. The remains of 153 Brigade had been sent to establish a defensive position at Le Havre so that what remained could not

A war artist's impression of the war in France, May 1940. Edward R Ardizzone's "On the Road to Louvain".

Another drawing from the same period by the same artist illustrating the difficulties of language within the 'auld alliance'.

have exceeded 2500 actual fighting men. The remainder must have been second echelon troops, service corps and others.

Further, the state of exhaustion these infantrymen were in is almost impossible to describe. For six weeks – from the time they went into the Saar in front of the Maginot – they had never had the opportunity to rest properly, to get off their clothes or even their boots. There had been no new clothing or equipment issued and very few reinforcements had arrived. Those that had come to strengthen the numbers were invariably inexperienced and only half-trained.

If anyone would like to get an idea of what this situation was really like let them try marching ten to twelve miles a day, digging a foxhole every night or day alternately, while carrying a rifle or Bren gun, ammunition, gas respirator and haversack of small kit and at the same time fighting on average on alternate days. There were no beds, not even chairs to sit on, no shelter and no proper periods of rest or meal times. It is not possible in peacetime to simulate the effect of such a

period of almost daily shelling, rifle and machine-gun fire, while after the move up from Rouen to the Bresle the Stuka dive bombers were in action against us daily – sometimes several times a day. Men fell asleep standing on their feet so long as they could rest their heads on something – a wall, the parapet of a bridge, the side of a truck.

By the time June 12, 1940 had arrived and the Division was in position at St Valery most of the men were far too exhausted to care very much what happened to them. All the same it must be emphasised that until the last day the thought of capitulation never entered their heads. When, at 0800 hrs the French surrendered and in the next two hours the handover to the Germans was completed as the surrender orders were issued to the individual battalions in the Division, there were mixed feelings and hope that, despite events, all might not be over.

This feeling of hope was something that was always to the forefront of many minds during the ensuing five years of imprisonment."

Stalag XXB

The library in Stalag XXB,
Willenberg.

Inset: Stalag XXB. Company
Sergeant Major James Fulton,
British 'Man of Confidence' and
the main go-between the
prisoners and their captors.

BUT I ASSURE YOU, MY DEAR CHAP — I REALLY AM FATHER CHRISTMAS!

Left: General Fortune saying goodbye to the men of his captured Division entraining en route to a German POW Camp in June 1940.

Bottom left: Christmas Card sent from POW camps in 1940.

Top right: Captain L Maclean presenting the shield to the winners of the Elbing Football League, at the sports held on July 2, 1944.

Centre right: Sports Day at Willenberg.

Bottom right: Elbing sports, July 2, 1944.

The Germans wasted no time in moving their prisoners out of the immediate area of St Valery. It was the start of a long march – up to 15 miles a day – towards Germany and Stalag XXB.

Douglas Thow remembers:
"If we were lucky we were given a cup of black coffee and a piece of bread. On many days there was no food at all and we were forced to forage in fields where there were potatoes, sugar beet, dandelions and nettles. Many of us had nettle soup, but often the beet and the potatoes were eaten raw. As we got into the populated areas the civilians were kind to us – except the North Belgians who spat at us – giving us a little food. We had only the clothes we stood up in and these were often soaked. We had to wash as best we could – in the puddles usually.

"There were some terrible sights to be seen in the areas we passed through. Gruesome sights. Mutilated bodies – arms and legs blown or hanging off – men lying or sitting where they had been hit. Corpses of all nationalities – whole villages flattened. It must have been like that during World War 1.

"When we reached Holland we were herded on to barges. For three days it was sheer hell as we were carried down the Scheldt Canal to Hemer in Germany. For the journey we were packed in below like slaves. We weren't allowed up for any reason."

When they reached Germany the prisoners were put into cattle trucks destined for one of the German POW camps in Poland. The trip took almost three days with men cramped together, unable to stretch or bend their limbs. Some soldiers never completed the journey. They died, propped up between their comrades. In the POW camp at Thorn in Poland the men were photographed, along with thousands of prisoners of all nationalities, given POW numbers and issued with identity discs. They were then allowed to send a postcard to their next-of-kin and any remaining possessions, such as soap and valuables, were taken from them.

However, their stay at Thorn, where at least they were being given better food – the bread ration was increased to two slices a day and there were bowls of soup – was to be a short one. Arrangements were being made by the Germans to draft the prisoners to various places – to work on Silesian farms, on road-making projects or, the most feared fate of all, labour in the Polish salt mines.

James Fulton, a Company sergeant major in the 2nd Battalion Seaforth Highlanders, who was later to become the man responsible for liaison between the prisoners and the German authorities at Stalag XXB, told the Germans he was an agricultural worker, expecting that life on a farm would ensure some additional food, if nothing else. It was not to be long before he regretted his mistaken belief.

"It was far from being an easy number. All we possessed was the clothing we stood up in. Ten of us shared two towels, one handkerchief and three razors. We were given billets in the unlit garret of the village school and were taken to a barn to get hay to sleep on. Winter was extremely cold after that harvest. The working day was from 5am to 7pm and in the winter we used to arrive in the fields in darkness and await daybreak before starting to dig potatoes or pull and dress turnips. The food was far from good. The main meal consisted of potatoes and milk soup and this ruined our bladders. Every one of us would consequently wake up five or six times in the night to make use of a stinking herring barrel in our sleeping quarters."

Eventually, his stint on the farm came to an end and Fulton was moved back to Stalag XXB near Marienburg where Douglas Thow had now been transferred after labouring on an autobahn project. There were many thousands of prisoners in Stalag XXB – British, French, Polish, Yugoslavs and, later, Italians. James Fulton began to make his presence known. A highly experienced soldier, he recognised that if morale was to be maintained among the prisoners then some form of link had to be made between them and the Germans so that welfare was not ignored. The men appointed him as their 'Man of Confidence' *(Vertraudeman)* and gradually the Germans accepted him as the voice of the prisoners when it came to dealing with such matters as the distribution of Red Cross parcels and the general administration of prisoners' needs.

A monthly camp magazine was started. Called the *Willenburg Echo* it was printed in Marienburg and contained photographs and items of news from Britain – information with no propaganda value such as countryside notes, football results and stories about film stars. There was also a Who's Who of camp personalities.

As POW camps go Stalag XXB was something approaching a model of its kind. Although strictly administered by the Germans the discipline was not, for the main part, of the harsh, brutal kind so frequently encountered in other similar establishments. When not engaged on work tasks the men had plenty of time to themselves which they passed in playing football – there were teams from England, Scotland, Wales, France and Belgium competing in an international tournament – digging their own swimming pool, staging Highland Games, and studying. Arrangements were made for the prisoners to continue their education and to take examinations for additional professional qualifications. The prisoners built their own concert hall and theatre where dozens of plays were produced over the years by Norman Wylie from Aberdeen who also assisted James Fulton as an interpreter in his dealings with the Germans.

Douglas Thow worked for a time in a fish shop in Marienburg.

"I was there for about four months. It wasn't too bad at all, despite a two mile march from the camp to the shop. This cushy number ended when the Germans caught us stealing fish. We had been doing it regularly, hiding fish in our dixie cans and taking them back to camp for the lads to cook. The Germans suspected something, but we always denied it until one day when they forced us to turn out our dixie cans. I got five days solitary

Above: Dance Band, main camp, Willenberg.

Above right: Post and parcel staff, main camp – Marienburg.

Right: Working Party 460, Losendorf, June 1944.

confinement in the bunker for this and after that, when I was released, I went to work in the Red Cross warehouse distributing clothing."

There were several escapes from Stalag XXB, mainly from working parties outside the camp, and many attempts which occasionally ended in disaster. Two men who made it were Bobby Easterbrook and Harold Johnson. After reaching Britain, via Sweden, Easterbrook sent a letter to the commandant of the POW camp who immediately sent for James Fulton and flourished it in front of him saying: "Now you know where Easterbrook is." Fulton had always flatly denied knowing of any plan by Easterbrook to escape or where he could be.

There were various ways of receiving escape material. James Fulton's main source was through next-of-kin parcels. "These parcels arrived at Marienburg and were checked under the supervision of the Germans. It often happened that we received parcels incorrectly addressed belonging to POW's of another Stalag. These were put into a small store without being checked so that they could be forwarded. Occasionally a parcel addressed to, say, Private Brown and

bearing no POW number would arrive. Knowing that it might contain something useful it was placed in the store. The usual German thoroughness failed to notice that the only person holding a key to the store was RQMS Tommy Primrose who was in charge of the Parcel Department.

"When an item was required to assist in an escape attempt we would go to the store and put it into a satchel I always carried with me in the camp. Holding the position I did I was never searched on returning in the evenings with my Stalag Parcel and Letter staff. On the few occasions a new guard attempted to do so I would shout 'Vertraudeman'. If that didn't do the trick, knowing the fear the average German soldier had for his superiors, I would say, 'Come with me to the Hauptman'. That was sufficient and my heart would then start to beat normally again."

Meanwhile, as the men of the old Highland Division adjusted themselves to life behind barbed wire in Germany, back in Britain a new 51st Highland Division was being moulded into shape ready for action with the Eighth Army under Montgomery in the Western Desert.

Top left: Helping to pass the time in Stalag XXB – the inevitable amateur dramatics in 'drag'.

Bottom left: 'French without Tears,' Stalag XXB, 1943

Above: Funeral of L/Cpl. MacFarlane, Black Watch, in Stalag XXB. By this stage of the war it was almost impossible in Germany to obtain wood for making coffins or crosses.

A New Phoenix

C. E. Lucas Phillips said in an extract from his book *Alamein:*

Of the British infantry, on the 51st Highland Division was to fall the largest part of the Alamein fighting. It was the only one at full strength. Freshly out from home in August, the 'Jocks' had learned their desert fighting technique by sending contingents into the line with the Australians, for whom they had a great admiration – a sentiment which the Aussies warmly returned.

The division came out to the desert with the memory of a tragedy to avenge against Rommel himself. In a last effort to stem the disasters of the Battle of France in 1940, 51st Division, led by Victor Fortune, but operating under French command, had been trapped at St Valery during Rommel's lightning drive through a broken country and obliged to surrender. From the ashes of the old division a new phoenix had arisen, eager to wipe out that unhappy record. The commander of the division was Douglas Wimberley, very tall and lean, tremendously energetic, a 'serious' soldier, but eager and cheerful in spirit. Riding in a jeep, with his long legs tucked up under his chin, covered with desert sores and wearing the bonnet of the Camerons, he was always happiest when right in front with his troops, never bothering about his food, and leaving his able GSO 1, Roy Urquhart to run divisional headquarters. His whole being was devoted to his division and, despite his English surname, he was an ardent Highlander. He was known affectionately as 'Big Tam' or 'Tartan Tam'. He believed in the outward and visible signs of corporate pride as a stimulus to the inner springs and he made sure that, wherever 51st Division went in its long trail of battle, the world should know that it had passed that way. It was a duty of his Military Police to write large the simple divisional emblem of HD all along that honourable trail.

This was something quite new to the Eighth Army, who had been bred in "security" measures and who chaffingly christened Wimberley's men "the Signwriters" or "the Highway Decorators". "Security", in this matter, went overboard; as Wimberley said, "Scottish troops always proclaim themselves . . ."

The roar of the barrage filled and overshadowed all thought and feeling . . .

Piper Macdonald of the Seaforths leads a section during a march in the Western Desert. The kilt was not usually worn in action but the odd skean dhu is in evidence.

In 51st Division, the kilted pipers, erect and proud beside their battalion and company commanders, broke into their wild-sweet music, heard shrill and high above the crash of shells, carrying the melodies of loch and glen across the foreign desolation. On their flanks the Australians and the New Zealanders, too, heard the heartening strains and knew thereby that, though the Jocks had vanished into the dust and the darkness, they were there.

"All my thoughts", said Robert Weir, of the Cameron Highlanders, "were pleasant thoughts; and when our piper played *The Road to the Isles* I asked myself: 'I wonder if it is'." For he knew that "the Isles" were the celestial islands of the Blest. Piper Duncan McIntyre, in Blair-Imrie's company of 5th Black Watch, nineteen years old, hit quickly twice, continued to play, but a third hit brought him to the ground. Dying, he still continued to play and, when his body was found, the bag was still in his oxter and his fingers still upon the chanter*.

Alamein – by C. E. Lucas Phillips.
(White Lion Publishers Ltd)

Right: Prime Minister Winston Churchill with Major General Wimberley, MC, GOC and General Alan Brooke during his visit to the Division in the Western Desert, August 24, 1942.

Below: General Montgomery inspecting a guard of Gordon Highlanders in 1942.

Below right: Piper Flett of the Seaforths, from the Isle of Fletta in the Orkneys, stops to have a chat with a Gordon Bren Carrier September 1942.

Left: 'The Ladies from Hell' go over the top. Men of the Highland Division training in the Desert. *Damen aus Helle* was the German soubriquet for the soldiers of the HD in WW1 when kilts were worn in action.

Below: The wartime caption says simply, "A 'Scotch Haircut' in the Desert".

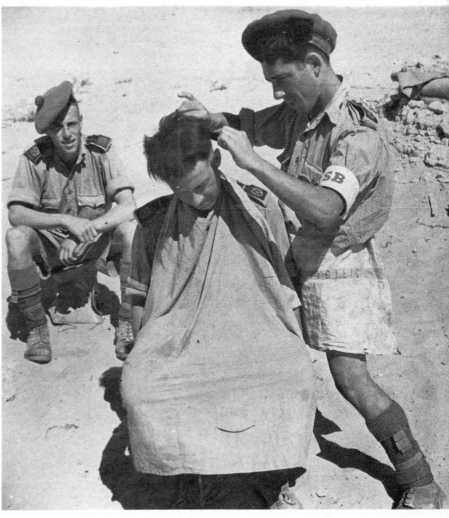

This well known photograph is almost certainly posed and shows Jocks of the Division running past a knocked-out German tank. The photograph is, however, genuine enough in its evocation of the sand, dust, smoke and sweat and the whole ambience of war in the Desert at the time of Alamein.

The Battle of Alamein – The Jocks
"Mak Siccar"

Stanzas of a poem by Hamish Henderson
reproduced from "Elegies for the Dead",
published by John Lehman of London,
1945

(a) The Waiting

Armour has foregathered, shuffling
through tourbillions of fine dust
The Crews don't speak much. They've had
last brew-up before battle. The tawny
deadland lies in silence
not yet smashed by salvoes.
No sound reaches us
from the African constellations.
The low ridge too is quiet
But no fear we're sleeping,
no need to remind us
that the nervous fingers of the searchlights
are nearly meeting and time is flickering
and this I think in a few minutes
while the whole power crouches for the spring.
X-20 in thirty seconds. Then begin

(b) the barrage

Let loose (rounds)
the exultant bounding hell-harrowing of sound.
Break the batteries. Confound
the damnable domination: Slake
the crashing breakers – hurled rubble of the guns.
Dithering darkness, we'll wake you! Hells bells
blind you. Be broken, bleed
deathshead blackness!
The thongs of the livid
firelight lick you
jagg'd splinters send you
underground
we'll bomb you, doom you, tomb you into grave's mound

(c) The Jocks

They move forward into no man's land, a vibrant sounding board.
As they advance
the guns push further murderous music
Is this all they will hear, this raucous apocalypse?
The spheres knocking in the night of Heaven?
The drummeling of overwhelming Niagra?
No! For I can hear it! Or is it? . . .tell
me that I can hear it! Now – listen.

Yes, hill and shieling
sea-loch and island, hear it, the yell
of your war-pipes, scaling sound's mountains
guns thunder drowning in their roaring swell!
– The barrage gulfs them: they're gulfed in the clumbering guns.
gulfed in gloom, gloom. Dumb in the blunderbuss black –
lost – gone in the anonymous cataract of noise.
Now again! The shrill war-song: it flaunts
aggression to the sullen desert. It mounts, it's scream
tops the Valkyrie, tops the colossal artillery.

Into the Desert

Italian paratroops captured in the Desert. They were used as infantry in the front line and officered by Germans. Their morale was low, much of their equipment very poor, and they were glad to be out of the war.

Brigadier Charles N. Barker (1st Battalion Gordon Highlanders) remembers:

"By a curious twist of fate I was commissioned into the Gordon Highlanders just before the outbreak of war, instead of entering the Royal Navy, an ambition which had been a boyhood dream. As an Englishman with no knowledge of Scotland, let alone the clans I was to serve with the 51st from October 1939 until the end of hostilities in May, 1945. This may indeed be a unique record because I think few infantry officers served in all theatres with the Division. It was both a rewarding and an unforgettable experience.

So, I started off as a second Lieutenant commanding thirty Scotsmen under the careful eye of Sgt Geary from Fraserburgh and CSM Courage, a man whose actions always reflected his name. These were real men from whom I learned so much when, quite frankly, I was still no more than a young lad; how to work a shovel, how to harden oneself against the most unpleasant conditions of weather and war, how to keep going when everything inside said "stop", how to mix with men and understand what made the Scottish fighting soldier tick; and how to lead men in war. I buried Sgt Geary after he had been riddled by machine-gun fire in the Bois de Cambron while obeying my first battle order. Before I was twenty-one years old I had to write to his young widow. Facing tasks such as this one's youth vanished overnight; war was a serious, frightening tough business but one's thermostat seemed to adjust to it in a most remarkable way after the initial shock.

I was wounded before the Division was encircled at St Valery and was caught up in a massive medical evacuation from Rouen to La Baule, finally running the gauntlet of Stukas on the SS *Batory*, a Polish liner, out of St Nazaire destined for Plymouth. We were luckier than those aboard the ill-fated *Lancastria*.

I can remember just before embarking at St Nazaire being ordered to leave my valise behind and stripping off my battle-dress trousers and pants and proudly donning my kilt, much to the amusement of many men and women on the quayside. Prior to this there had been a very strong lobby within the Division in favour of fighting in the kilt, in my opinion an unsuitable garment for modern warfare.

Serious consideration was given to the provision of "Drawers, Highland Anti-Gas for the use of" which were in some unlikely Highland manner to be rolled

down from under the kilt to be hitched over one's nose on the warning, "Gas". But both factions – for and against – carried on their campaigns in good humour and it was just part of that tremendous spirit that I have never known to be equalled.

In the reformed Division every officer and man was imbued with a tremendous price in the achievements of the past and a desire to avenge St Valery, fostered whole-heartedly by a new dynamic chieftain, Douglas Wimberley. He was not endeared overmuch to the English, but in some odd way I survived and as Carrier Platoon Commander under Horatius Murray landed in North Africa after six weeks in the troopship *Empress of India*. Horatius Murray, later to become a General, was affectionately known as "Nap" Murray because of his bald head

and somewhat rotund appearance which make him look like Napoleon.

The desert was something quite new to all of us. So, after an acclimatising period at Quassassin Camp I was sent up to the front to learn desert warfare from the extremely tough 9th Australian Division. I well remember my first meeting. "Hello, Limey – coming out on patrol tonight?" I was under test. "Of course", I replied – and I was in. However, a few hours later I was horrified when I heard their ploy for that night – to penetrate an area of 'no man's land' for about two thousand yards to locate a crashed Desert Airforce fighter, then to hitch it to an enormous Scammell Recovery vehicle and tow it back behind the lines. What a night that was.

Every step we took with this vast vehicle grinding beside us, bumping its way ever closer to the enemy lines, made

Top left: Soldiers of the Division running through the smoke and dust of enemy shell fire.

Centre left: Two wounded men of the Black Watch being attended by a medical orderly.

Bottom left: Four 'Jocks' 'dug in' in a forward position after their initial advance from El Alamein.

Above: A range finder being operated from a Brigade HQ during the Battle of Alamein, October 1942.

47

'Jocks' in a Bren Gun Carrier
examine the remains of a
German Mark IV Special tank
destroyed by Engineers.
November 1942.

Right: Jocks examining a
captured Spandau machine
gun, November 1942.

me certain that before long the wrath of the enemy would be unleashed upon us for our sheer audacity. The aircraft had been lying in this area of the desert for some time and had been used by both sides as a mortar and artillery marker. If Jerry heard us he would have no difficulty in ranging on us because we were moving directly through the target area. There was no cover in the flat, open desert on that star-studded night. Every sound from that engine and winch sounded to me like Big Ben – the whole operation seemed an eternity. All the same we made it successfully, without a shot being fired. As a result one more aircraft was repairable to be used in the Battle of El Alamein that was soon to take place over that ground.

I learned many lessons on the peculiarities of desert warfare from the Australians and returned to the Division to be sent to the boxes near Alam el Halfa among the ruins of Rommel's panzers. We practised our desert warfare skills, perfected our compass marches by day and night using the desert compass. We learned to live on a minimum of water, to brew up in desert fires made of sand and petrol, to compete with the swarm of flies that stung and bit and entered one's mouth with every spoonful, to protect ourselves from the scorching sun by day and the bitter cold at night and to deal with the dangers and agonies of desert sores and "gippy" tummy and the importance of searching our boots and clothing for scorpions. Perhaps the hardest lesson of all to learn was to enjoy a regular diet of hardtack, bully and "V" cigarettes.

All this time planning was well advanced for the greatest battle of the desert. Soon we were drawn into practising our role in the desert, first as a Battalion, then on Brigade and Divisional level. At first we trained with no fire, then later live artillery fire was used. During one of the late night practices I was hit in the mouth by a piece of shrapnel and in no time my lip was a large, unpleasant festering mess. Once again I landed in medical hands and was evacuated to a Delta hospital to have the damage repaired and then out to a Reinforcement Camp in the Canal Zone.

At this time I had only one object in mind which, perhaps on reflection, illustrates the tremendous morale that existed in the Division at this time. I knew that the great day was rapidly approaching when we were to fling ourselves against the German line. I knew my role in that battle; the only thought in my head was to get up to the desert as

quickly as possible and rejoin the Division. I raised the question with the Commandant and his reply was, "No, you stay here as a first reinforcement." I immediately wrote to 'Nap' Murray, my CO, and told him the position. His reply came by return, instructing me to pack my kit and be at a certain map reference at midnight where a truck from the battalion would pick me up. Sure enough, it was there and I was on my way to the front once again, completely oblivious of the consternation my absence was causing at the Reinforcement Camp.

We negotiated large boulders and drove out on to a track, the wheels of the vehicle throwing up a mass of the finest dust which caked on our sweat. The track was now a vast dust bowl getting wider as more and more vehicles used it. We were cocooned, fine dust was everywhere; inches deep. "Yes" – the driver knew where to take me; "No" – we weren't yet at the Front. Eventually, when it was almost dark, he arrived at his destination and we motored towards a cluster of camouflaged vehicles. But there was no sign of life and after ten minutes or so of searching for someone the truth dawned on me. The Battalion had already left for their assembly position and we were among dummy vehicles made of hessian screening, part of an elaborate deception plan to keep the Germans guessing.

It took many more hours of searching

Sappers of the Division defusing German 'S' mines. These anti-personnel mines contained 260 pieces of shrapnel and went off under very slight pressure.

50

Left: Major General Wimberley discussing plans with his GSO1, Col Urquhart (later Commander at Arnhem) and his signal officers Lt Col Denholm-Young from Edinburgh and Captain Fraser from Kirkcaldy during the advance from El Alamein, November 1942.

Below: Officers of the Division interrogating a German prisoner. November 1942.

before I was able to report to my CO at the Front. The Battalion was well dug-in in highly camouflaged positions and forbidden to move from their 'doovers' (slit trenches) during the hours of daylight. For a number of days we baked in the intense heat and this period can be remembered for its days of what seemed to be extraordinary length and for the endless waiting for the order to move forward. Meanwhile, I had been posted as a deserter but this was put right by General Montgomery who tersely remarked that he did not know how it was possible for one to desert from the rear – to the front.

At 2135 hrs on October 23, 1942 we moved forward to the accompaniment of wave upon wave of thunderous gunfire. The skyline behind us was suddenly ablaze as shells tore apart the night to turn what had been an uneasy peace into the chaos of war. The smell of cordite intermingled with the grit and dust stirred up by thousands of bursting projectiles a few hundred yards ahead, the clean air became foul as we paced out on compass bearings to our objectives deep in the enemy lines.

My particular task was to move forward with 5/7ths Gordons Command Post and once they had hit their objective, to retrace my steps to the start-line along a white tape running through the minefields so that our vital support weapons could be brought forward. I was to lead the column through three or four minefields, bear right 90 degrees until I hit the 5th Black Watch tape and then follow it on until I reached the 1st Gordons who, by which time, should have leap-frogged beyond 5th Black Watch to their "Aberdeen" feature.

Once on the 5/7th objective I bid farewell to Roscoe Saunders, their CO and with one escort and a .38 pistol with eighteen rounds of ammunition, retraced my steps along the white tape laid by the 5/7th Gordons as their centre line. You can well imagine my surprise to suddenly find myself in the company of hordes of Italian soldiers fully armed, any one of whom could have shot me without trace. I quickly realised there was no point in doing more than encourage as best I could this host of prisoners to follow me down the tape as the shelling from both directions whistled overhead, many

falling unpleasantly close to us. We moved cautiously back through each minefield, clearly marked on the German side, *Achtungminen*. There were seven in all and eventually we reached the first of the sappers hard at it clearing the lanes to bring the transport through.

Men were detailed to take charge of the prisoners who were only too willing to surrender and get out of the way and at the entrance to the first minefield was the head of my Brigade column of support weapons, including our vital anti-tank guns. When dawn broke we had to dig these in to meet the enemy counter-attack and after several hours we started to move forward again as each minefield was gapped.

As we moved on slowly the hope was in everyone's mind that each gap might have been cleared properly as the tyres of our vehicle were biting deeply into the sand. Every so often a large yellow and orange

flash would tell us if a mine had been missed during the clearance operations. Tracer from anti-aircraft guns continued to fire, giving a guide to direction, and enemy shelling sought to range on the gaps between which I searched for the vital white tape. The strain was considerable, eyes constantly focused on the ground, ears pitched for the sound of shells, trying to judge how close they were landing, always trying to keep one's feelings in check.

We snaked our way forward until the seventh gap was cleared by 2330 hrs, then off we forked at right-angles, hoping against hope that the 5th Black Watch tape would be showing clearly among the debris and that no other minefields lay ahead. At length we found the tape, followed it, dropped off the 5th Black Watch support weapons, then pressed on into the night to contact the 1st Gordons.

In the thick of it was that indomitable man, my CO 'Nap' Murray who immediately gave me details of a particularly gruelling task he wanted me to do. The Battalion's leading companies, 'A' and 'C' had disappeared into the darkness to 'Aberdeen', the Battalion objective, and no contact had been made with them since their departure. 'B' Company had endeavoured to go to their left and had been held up by heavy enemy fire and minefields. As a result they were pinned down.

I was ordered to take a carrier patrol forward in the dead of night to find 'A' and 'C' Coy. and then report back. So began the most hazardous and frightening journey of my life. Realising that to move carriers forward during darkness without extreme care was the height of stupidity I dismounted and told three carriers to follow as I went forward on foot. After fifty or sixty yards I hit a wire beyond which was a track runningly slightly to the left.

Jocks moving forward from El Alamein.

New vehicle marks were clearly visible so I moved the carriers over the wire and on to the vehicle tracks. I had hit a German minefield gap, any movement off which was fraught with danger. As we were moving carefully down the gap there was clearly heard above the general rumble of the battle, a shattering crash from the left. German 88mm guns had opened up on us.

I gave the sign to the driver to get a move on and we ran a gauntlet of fire the entire length down the gap. We could see the gun flashes as they followed us. An 88mm engages you unlike other shelling; you only hear the shell coming after the strike. It is a very odd and terrifying situation. Fortunately, we got through without any carrier being hit and emerged at the end deep into enemy territory. On leaving the gap we bore right and swung along the minefield wire searching for 'A' and 'C' Coy, but found no sign of them. We circled an old oil drum which later was discovered to be located very close to the east end of the kidney feature – the Battalion objective 'Aberdeen'. Small arms fire sent us back retracing our tracks which were quite visible in the sand. Once more we were very soon in the thick of it again.

The noise was appalling. Everything seemed to be aimed at us. When well down the corridor we saw a wounded Gordon on our left. We stopped and quickly grabbed him, put him aboard a carrier and pressed on. He was from 'C' Coy and had been lying there for some time. In a hail of fire we eventually returned to the Battalion Command Post having failed in our mission. All the same we had found a vital gap through the enemy minefield, had been on the 'Aberdeen' feature and could report that this had not been captured. The missing companies were short of their objective. This was important information. We were told to dig in and await daylight. This did not take long; in the desert there is very little twilight or dawn.

The next day began with the biggest firework display one could ever wish to see. The whole Panzer Army engaged the full armoured might of the Eighth Army while we kept our heads down, caught in the middle between them. Armoured piercing tracer shells streaked across the desert in the most gigantic tank battle to date. Eventually we managed to find the decimated remains of 'A' and 'C' Coy and as opportunity offered moved forward in our carriers to bring in the wounded. The only officer unhurt and commanding the remnants was Captain Harry Gordon.

One of the wounded that day was 'Nap' Murray, our gallant CO.

One is sometimes asked whether Faith helps in the thick of battle. Of course it does; faith in your pals, faith in your commanders and for those given the gift to trust the unseen, faith when walking through the valley of the shadow of death. I pondered the future as I thumbed my Bible just before the Battle of El Alamein and my eyes fell on this phrase: "Thou shalt not die but live, that thou mayest praise the name of the Lord." Sometime after, when lying in hospital in Cairo after being flung twenty-five yards by a German landmine near Marsa Brega, I returned to that passage and in amazement read the next verse; "The Lord hath chastened thee sore but He hath not given thee over unto death."

Above: General Wimberley using a wireless set during the latter stage of the advance on Tripoli, January 1943.

Above right: The parade and march past of the Division during the visit of Prime Minister Winston Churchill to Tripoli, February 1943.

Right: Covered by a Bren gun section, a patrol of the Black Watch moves in to Marsa Brega.

Machine-gunners of 1 Bn
Middlesex Regiment putting
down harassing fire in support
of forward elements in Goch.
February 19, 1945.

Machine Gun Battalion

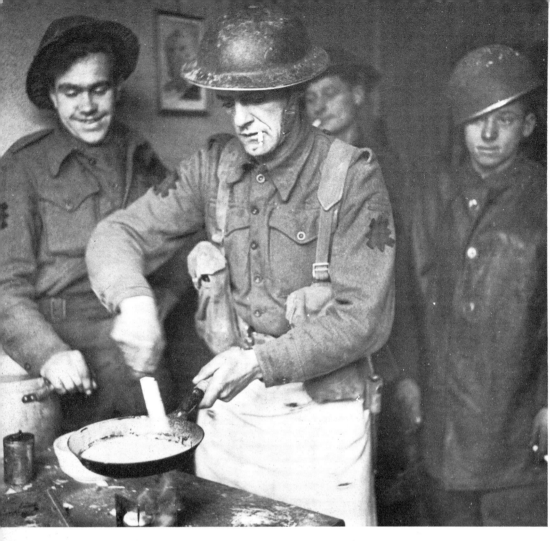

The 1st/7th Battalion The Middlesex Regiment were posted to the 51st Highland Division as Machine Gun Battalion in October, 1941. Coming from London they were at first regarded with a little suspicion and much curiosity by the Highland troops. From their station at Ballater and Crathie, in Aberdeenshire, they carried out a number of winter exercises with the various brigades.

The battalion sailed to Egypt in early 1942 with Divisional Headquarters and the 7th Battalion The Black Watch on the *Stratheden*. Their first main engagement as part of the Division was the Battle of Alamein.

In this battle and for the whole of the Desert, Sicily and North West Europe campaigns 'B' Company from Enfield supported 154th Brigade consisting of The Black Watch and the Argyll and Sutherland Highlanders.

'C' Company from Hornsey supported 153rd Brigade made up of Gordon Highlanders and The Black Watch.

'D' Company from Tottenham supported 152nd Brigade consisting of Seaforth Highlanders and Cameron Highlanders.

'A' Company from Highgate was at El Alamein and in many subsequent engagements attached to the 7th Battalion The Black Watch. It also came under the command of the 23rd Armoured Brigade for the various Spear, Hammer, etc, pursuit forces.

Through to the end of the war the Middlesex Regiment stayed with the Highland Division as their machine-gunners and one account of their activities was written by Captain James Borthwick, an observer officer who saw the Division in action in the Western Desert, North Africa and Sicily.

In a despatch to a newspaper he wrote:
"It was the red hair that first attracted my attention.
'You're not a Scot, are you?', I asked.
The young officer looked up and grinned.
'Why not?' he replied.

He was Lieutenant Roderick McPherson, from Dron, Bridge of Earn in Perthshire, the only Scot in the Middlesex Regiment, the only English regiment in the reformed Highland Division.

But there was a reason for it. Roderick McPherson had been trained as a machine gunner with the Malayan Volunteer Force and at the outbreak of war had returned to Britain to join up.

Above left: After a night of counter-attacks by the Germans and heavy shelling and mortaring, Pte Fred (Sunny) Barton of Balham, London and the Black Watch 'borrowed' some flour from somewhere and a frying pan and still complete in fighting kit, got on with the job of making pancakes for Shrove Tuesday.

Being a machine-gunner he was commissioned into the Middlesex.

For the Middlesex are all Cockneys. They wear the side hat, they have a brass band, they lay no claim to the kilt. But they are as proud of the HD as any of the kilted regiments.

'The Middies – they're the wee boys with the guts', say the Jocks of the kilted regiments, and well they have proved it.

I never forget my first sight of them at Alamein trudging on behind the infantry carrying eighty pounds of machine-gun equipment on their backs. And on the way to Tripoli when the Black Watch were in parlous plight in The Hills of Homs it was the Middlesex machine-gunners who hiked their way over the wadis and hills, man-handling their heavy machine-guns to open up in time to save the day.

For the Middlesex have a reputation second to none as infantry in the last war; and even in this, when put to it, they have shown that they have lost none of their skill.

It was in the closing stages of the Sicilian battle. The Middlesex had gone forward to occupy a hill they had been assured was clear of the enemy.

Lt Rampling walked over the crest to find himself face to face with two Germans. He fired his revolver at them and got back. There were Germans all around. One band was only twenty-five yards away from a Middlesex post. The Middies couldn't fire on them for the ridge.

'Cover me' said Corporal Fred Dean and crawled forward. Lance Corporal Sidney Mundy kept his eye and his rifle on the Germans. Corporal Dean got within twenty yards and jumped to his feet and rushed into the post. Then discovered to his horror that his tommy gun had jammed. Nothing daunted, he used it as a club and the Germans were dealt with. Eighty prisoners were taken in a few hours by such forays. And then the Middlesex settled down to their machine-guns again."

Roderick McPherson, referred to by Captain Borthwick in his newspaper despatch, was killed at Eindhoven in Holland on the eve of his promotion from captain to Major. Although Captain Borthwick mentions his training with the Malayan Volunteer Force he did, in fact, come voluntarily from South Africa to join the British Army while his elder brother, Ian, fought with the South African forces.

Vickers machine guns of the Middlesex Regiment give supporting fire to the advancing infantry. February 1945.

Letters from North Africa

No 2884169 Cpl G. Mackie:
I am fit and well, only troubled by flies and mosquitoes. There are plenty of them here, also plenty of sunshine. It's lovely weather in this country. I am getting a nice tan on with sunbathing. I'll show it off when I come home. You were asking how we feed. Well, we do our own cooking. Each carrier has its own utensils and we are issued out rations every day. We enjoy this very much. We can manage to make a few tasty bits besides. We usually get plenty of eggs to buy from the natives' farms, as you would call it, and sometimes pick up some fresh vegetables, so we don't do so badly at all for food. Now for the other side of the story. We are normally in bed at 8.30 and up at first light. There's no 'lights out' – we go to bed when it gets dark. We are at Sfax in the meantime; we were first to enter the town; my carrier was second in the lead. We got a great welcome. French flags were hoisted, flowers were thrown on the carriers and the youngsters piled on to the carriers and showed us the way through the town. The cameraman was on the go, too, so I think our faces should be in the news.

No 2883512 Sgt J. Irving:
There is very little I can say, but pages I would like to fill. If I told you all I would like to, they would cut down the soldier's pay to employ more censors. Never mind, I am always grumbling, never satisfied; that's me. We had a pet in our team – a cockerel. We had it three days. It used to crow too early in the morning, so we had him cooked, and he was grand. I picked up a tortoise yesterday, it was a large one. He stayed about an hour and then walked away. Is our garden dug yet? I could apply for leave to dig it, but would they grant it? I think if I went and asked for a travelling warrant it would shake them up. This Army are shouting me on parade again, but they can wait. Drake finished his game of bowls, so Irving will finish his mail. Now, this letter is like our 'Duff' – a complete mix-up. I'm standing here writing, keeping an eye on the paper and one around me to see if anyone is around. The more you do the less thanks. All we want is 'bags of Brasso and Blanco'. Spit and polish always. I'm not in the dumps, but as happy as always.

No. 3661606 Pte E. Day:
I'm still going strong. The flies in this part of the country seem to be worse than those in Egypt, they certainly seem to bite harder. The only way to keep them off is to take our boots and socks off. We haven't yet decided which is the lesser of the two evils. We had quite a novel experience when entering a certain town. We were rather fortunate in being the first troops to enter, and what a welcome we got. A lot of the French women were weeping tears of joy, and the whole place was alive with flags. We were unlucky and had some job to get across a bad patch at the outskirts. However, we got going and then lost our way. One old fellow begged to show us the way, so we hoisted him up on top, flag as well, and away we went, the old chap waving his flag and singing 'It's a long way to Tipperary'. Then we were bombarded with flowers. It seemed as though thousands of them were sailing through the air. I have pressed a sprig of delphiniums in my pay book as a remembrance.

Far left: "... don't walk if you can ride."

Above: Seizing the opportunity of doing a little laundry.

61

Gordon Highlanders 'break
cover' for the official
photographer, Mareth, March
1943.

VC at Wadi Akarit

Above: Seaforth and Cameron Highlanders scramble down the steep sides of a wadi.

Top right: As part of the same sequence, the wartime caption tells us that 'Reaching the Wadi safely, they cross the stream to the opposite bank'.

Bottom right: . . . and here they are, on 'patrol'.

As the Eighth Army pressed on across North Africa, with Tripoli taken and Tunis lying before them, they reached a part of the coast line known as the Gabes Gap, a narrow strip of land heavily mined and with a massive anti-tank ditch overlooked by a bare ridge called Roumana. The job of breaking through the ditch and minefield and establishing a bridgehead, so that the rest of the Brigade could press through to engage the enemy, was given to the 7th Battalion Argyll and Sutherland Highlanders, commanded by Lt. Col Lorne Maclaine Campbell. This officer who had won the DSO for gallant leadership in France in 1940 and a bar to it for the part he had played in capturing important objectives during the Battle of El Alamein led his men in the attack upon the Wadi Akarit position on April 6, 1943 – an action that ended with him being awarded the Victoria Cross.

Announcing the award the official citation described the events of that memorable day:

"The attack had to form up in complete darkness and had to traverse the main offshoot of the Wadi Akarit at an angle to the line of advance.

In spite of heavy machine-gun and shell fire in the early stages of the attack, Lt Col Campbell successfully accomplished this difficult operation, captured at least 600 prisoners and led his battalion to its objective, having to cross an unswept portion of the enemy minefield in doing so.

Later, upon reaching his objective, he found that a gap which had been blown by the Royal Engineers in the anti-tank ditch did not correspond with the vehicle lane which had been cleared in the minefield. Realising the vital necessity of quickly establishing a gap for the passage of anti-tank guns, he took personal charge of the operation.

It was now broad daylight and, under very heavy machine-gun fire and shell fire, he succeeded in making a personal reconnaissance and in conducting operations which led to the establishing of a vehicle gap.

Throughout the day Lt Col Campbell held his position with his battalion in the face of extremely heavy and constant shell fire, which the enemy was able to bring to bear by direct observation.

About 16.30 hours determined enemy counter-attacks began to develop, accompanied by tanks. In this phase of the fighting Lt Col Campbell's personality dominated the battlefield by a display of valour and utter disregard for personal safety, which could not have been excelled.

Realising that it was imperative for the future success of the army plan to hold the bridgehead his battalion had captured, he inspired his men by his presence in the forefront of the battle, cheering them on and rallying them as he moved to those points where the fighting was heaviest.

When his left forward company was forced to give ground, he went forward alone, into a hail of fire, and personally reorganised their position, remaining with the company until the attack at this point was held.

As reinforcements arrived upon the scene, he was seen standing in the open directing the fight under close range fire of enemy infantry, and he continued to do so although already painfully wounded in the neck by shell fire.

It was not until the battle died down that he allowed his wound to be dressed.

Even then, although in great pain, he refused to be evacuated, remaining with

his battalion and continuing to inspire them by his presence on the field.

Darkness fell with the Argylls still holding their positions, though many of its officers and men had become casualties.

There is no doubt that but for Lt Col Campbell's determination, splendid example of courage and disregard of pain, the bridgehead would have been lost.

This officer's gallantry and magnificent leadership when his now tired men were charging the enemy with the bayonet and were fighting them at hand-grenade range, are worthy of the highest honour, and can seldom have been surpassed in the long history of the Highland Brigade."

The following day a war correspondent saw Lt Col Campbell wearing a bandage. His truck was parked just off the road. He was shaving.

"Have you been wounded?" he asked.

The Lt Colonel grinned and waved his razor.

"Oh no. Just cut myself with this."

Campaigning in Tunisia

A Gordon Highlander hanging out the washing on the Mareth Line!

Left: Cooling off after a spell in the Line.

Below: CQMS George Mitchell, (6th Black Watch), a Perth man who joined up in 1923, hands out the cigarette ration in the Desert in 1943.

Top left: An Italian prisoner being interrogated at Divisional HQ in March, 1943.

Centre left: What happens to a headquarters cook who is two seconds late with breakfast. March 1943.

Below: A narrow pass is held by the Gordon Highlanders in a hilly part of the Mareth Line. March 1943.

Left: General Wimberley attends one of General Montgomery's battle conferences. Next to him is General Bobby Erskine, commanding the 'Desert Rats'. March 1943.

Jocks aboard and a 6-pounder anti-tank gun in tow, a tank moves up. April, 1943.

Right: In the Desert war even the dentist was mobile.

Below: Soldier of the Black Watch going into action aboard a Valentine tank, April 1, 1943.

Bottom: Captain J. D. MacGregor, Black Watch, addressing his men on their role in co-operation with the tanks in the advance on Sfax, April 1943.

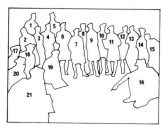

Commanders and Senior Staff Officers of the 51st Highland Division PLAN ALAMEIN, October 1942

1 Lt Col H. SAUNDERS
  5/7 Gordons

2 Lt Col L. CAMPBELL
  A & S.H
  (later Brig & V.C.)

3 Brig G. ELLIOT
  C.R.A.

4 Lt Col H. MURRAY (late Camerons)
  1st Gordons
  (later General Sir Horatius)

5 Lt Col R. MIERS
  5th Camerons

6 Lt Col T. RENNIE
  5th Black Watch.
  (later Maj-General),
  (Killed in action)

7 Brig D. GRAHAM
  Cameronians, 153 Bde
  (later Maj-General)

8 Lt Col T. THICKNESSE
  26th Fd Regt. R.A.
  (later Brig)
  (Killed in action)

9 Brig H. HOULDSWORTH
  Seaforth, 154 Bde
  (later Sir Henry &
  Lord Lieut of Moray.)

10 Lt Col R. URQUHART,
   H.L.I.
   G.S.O.I.
   (later Maj-General)

11 Brig G. MURRAY
   Seaforth, 152 Bde

12 Lt Col J. STIRLING
   5th Seaforth
   (later Brig & Lord Lieut of Nairn)

13 Lt Col W. ROPER – COLDBECK
   1st Black Watch

14 Lt Col J. SHIEL
   28th Fd Regt R.A.
   (later Brig)
   (Killed in action)

15 Lt Col J. STEPHENSON,
   7th MIDDX

16 Maj-General D. WIMBERLEY
   Camerons
   G.O.C. of 51st Highland Division

17 Col R. GALLOWAY
   A.D.M.S.
   (later Maj-General)

18 Lt Col J. COLAM,
   R.A.
   A & Q.

19 Lt Col E. GRANT
   A & S.H.
   Recce Bn
   (later Brig)

20 Lt Col K. MACKESSACK
   2nd Seaforth
   (later Vice Lieut of Moray.)

21 Lt Col J. OLIVER
   7th Black Watch
   (later Brig & Vice Lieut of Angus.)

Absent – Lt Col H. SUGDEN newly appointed C.R.E. (later Maj-General Sir Henry)

From a painting by Ian Eadie reproduced by permission of the Keeper, Scottish National Museum.

Yes, hill and shieling
sea-loch and island, hear it, the yell
of your war-pipes, scaling sound's mountains
guns thunder drowning in their roaring swell!

Jocks at El Alamein./Painting by Michael Stride

Piper E. J. Dawson, 7th Black
Watch. Painting by Ian Eadie
(By permission of the Dundee
Museum and Art Gallery)

Above: The 'Highway Decorators' at work – Jocks paint their Divisional Sign on a house in Sfax, April 1943.

Left: Long service Quartermasters serving with the 154 Bde, 51st Highland Division, in the Desert. Left to right front Captain John McNaughton, 1st Black Watch, from Dunfermline, Captain J Stapleton, 126 Field Regiment RA, of Arbroath; (left to right rear), Lt. Q/M A Leath, 1st Black Watch, of Kirkcaldy, Captain James McKechnie, 7th Black Watch, of Perth, and Captain James Richardson of the 7th Argylls from Stirling.

73

Germans and Italians surrendering after the battle of the Gabes Cap, April 6, 1943.

Right: The shower-bath unit finds a pleasantly shaded site among the palm trees at Makarouf in the spring of 1943.

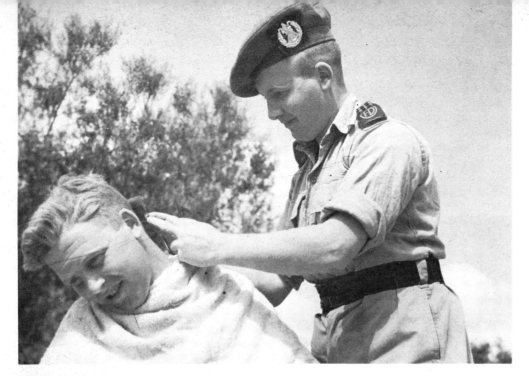

Top left: L/Cpl Leslie Thompson giving L/Cpl Douglas Thompson, his brother, a hair cut. Both the men were drivers for the CO of the 5th Camerons and came from Inverness. April 1943.

Centre left: Camerons in a domestic scene among the olive trees.

Below: Captain W Milne, Q/Master of the 5th Camerons, distributing the rum ration.

Above: Another Cameron Highlanders' superstition transferred to the Desert. After dropping coins into a specially made well, the wishers take a drink of water for good luck and health to follow them for the rest of the year. The tradition originated at Culloden.

Left: One of the mascots of 152 Brigade was 'Wee Willie', who was picked up as a lamb at Marsa Brega (Left to right) Captain Donald McKillop, Captain John Mitchell and Captain William Milne of the Camerons.

Top right: Bayonets fixed,
Cameron Highlanders on parade
just before the final battle in
Tunisia.

Centre right: Tunis Victory
Celebration. The massed pipes
and drums of the Division in the
procession, May 20, 1943.

Below: Drummers from the
Division in the same parade.

Above: Secretary of State for War, Sir James Grigg on a visit to the Division in North Africa in June 1943 seen here with General Alexander and General Wimberley.

Left: Will Fyfe, the great Scottish comedian, entertaining men of the Seaforth Highlanders in North Africa on July 5, 1943.

79

Verses from "TOWARDS THE EAST"
by Bernard Fergusson (now Lord Ballantrae)

Remote from pilgrimage, a dusty hollow
Lies in the Libyan plain:
And there my comrades sleep, who will not follow
The pipes and drums again:
Who followed closely in that desperate sally
The pipes that went before:
Who, heedless now of Muster or Reveille
Sleep sound for evermore,

In days of peace, when days of war were nearing,
My comrades who are dead
Once in a while looked up the dark track, peering
Where Fate and Glory led
For these, the chosen of their generation,
This was the path it took,
That ended in the sand and desolation
Ten miles beyond Tobruk

Far off in Scotland at the hour of battle,
As these her sons fell dead,
Above the herds of frosty breathing cattle
The winter sun rose red.
In every cothouse and in every city
In these remembered shires
The kettle sang its early morning ditty
On newly kindled fires.

To those dear houses with their chimneys reeking
In Angus or in Fife,
No spirit came its words of omen speaking,
To mother or to wife;
Yet in the homeless desert to the southward
Before the sun was high
The husbands whom they loved, the sons they mothered
Stood up and went to die

The night braids up her darkness like a curtain
The morning star grows pale,
Till suddenly the hope is sure and certain
That death cannot prevail;
And in my need my comrades send assurance
That breaks on me with day
That from the grave that sealed their long endurance
The stone is rolled away.

These verses from the book 'Lowland Soldier' are reproduced by kind permission of Lord Ballantrae. The poem is in memory of the 2nd Black Watch in their fight at Tobruk in November 1941, but the sentiments expressed might be applied to any of the three Black Watch battalions that fought in the Highland Division in North Africa a year or so later.

Graves of Seaforth Highlanders who fell in the fighting around Wadi Akarit and the Gabes Gap. April 1943.

Sicily Invasion. Landing operations begin. Troops of the Highland Division wading ashore.

The Conquest of Sicily

Top left: Pipers playing to men of 2nd Seaforth Highlanders aboard LCIs.

Left: A scene taken from the bridge of an LCI showing troops resting on the bow en route to Sicily.

Top centre: Men of the 2nd Seaforth Highlanders embarking on landing craft for the invasion of Sicily, July 1943.

Top right: The embarkation for Sicily begins – July 5th, 1943.

Right: General Montgomery chatting to Major Sym of 2nd Bn Seaforths before addressing some of the men taking part in the Sicily landings.

Top left: Invasion of Sicily. Officers of the 1st Black Watch discussing their part in the operations. In the centre is Lt Col C N Blair.

Centre left: Sicily Invasion – at least the Mediterranean was warm.

Below: The first prisoners – all Italians – are escorted to the landing beach for onward transit via landing craft to PoW camps in North Africa.

Above: Some rode ashore and arrived dry shod.

Left: A Sherman tank rumbles up the beach.

Right: Jocks wading ashore on July 6, 1943.

Far right top: – and moving inland.

Far right bottom: – to be followed by more and more. (The white marks on the Jocks' shoulders indicate where the wartime censor has attempted – in vain – to obliterate the HD signs.)

Left: The beaches at Cape Passero. Brigadier Gordon MacMillan commanding 152 Brigade of the Division, and Brigadier Ricky Richards, commanding 23rd Armoured, discuss the next move.

Below: Bren carriers towing anti-tank guns, moving forward in Sicily, July 1943.

Right: Two officers of the
Division, Major Keating and
Major Scot-Noble.

Above: Sicily. Italian prisoners going down to the beach after surrendering to 'Jocks' of the Division.

Centre left: Wounded HD soldiers during the fighting for Francofonte in Sicily being treated at the RAP before being sent to hospital.

Bottom left: Guns of the Division arriving at Noto. July 1943.

**Above: Entry Into Militello.
Bren carriers of the Division
passing through the streets of
Militello crowded with
cheering people. July 1943.**

**Left: A German officer, Captain
Gunter, OC No 2 Abteilung, 3rd
Paratroop Rifle Regiment, was
captured in civilian clothes
while trying to get through the
Allied lines near Buccheri,
Sicily. Captain Gunter is here
being questioned by Lt
Henderson an intelligence
officer of the 51st Highland
Division. July 1943.**

93

Top left: Another German prisoner exchanging photographs with his captors, July 21, 1943.

Left: Private Stanley Davies of the 5th Seaforths riding a captured pack mule. The swastika was branded on the unfortunate animal's neck.

Top centre: A German Tiger Mark VI tank found abandoned and blown up by the leading formations of the Division. The Tiger Mark VI with its 88mm gun weighed 72 tons and was of limited use on the narrow rock-walled roads of Sicily.

Top right: A celebrated non-smoker hands out the fags. General Montgomery passes over a consignment of cigarettes to General Wimberley for distribution to the Highland Division. July 25, 1943.

Right: A Scottish Sergeant Major samples some of the fruits of Sicily. The wartime caption observes: 'A picture which shows the complete accord with which British soldiers have been received by the people of Sicily. A Sergeant Major of the Highland Division held no terrors for these young Sicilians . . .'

On your way, brother, the War's still on out here...

Gordon Highlanders boarding landing craft at the East India docks, June 3, 1944.

"At Touffreville on June 12, 1944 (soon after the Normandy landing) the enemy attacked Battalion HQ at 0400 hours with three MG 34's, machine pistols and mortars.

"Sgt McPherson, the Provost Sgt, at once took over and organised the defensive fire of signallers, batmen and police. Completely regardless of his own safety he went from post to post controlling the fire amid a hail of enemy fire.

"The entrance to Battalion HQ was covered by an MG 34 firing on fixed line only ten yards from the gate. Sgt McPherson went forward against it by himself, armed with a 36 grenade and sten gun. He killed the gun crew and then silenced a sniper on a nearby roof-top. This high degree of offensive spirit, initiative and leadership won for Battalion HQ the fire fight and forced the enemy, after considerable casualties, to withdraw.

"Sgt McPherson's conduct was an inspiration to all around him."

This was the terse, official language of the citation awarding the Military Medal to 2885102 Sgt William Blackhall McPherson of the 5/7th Gordon Highlanders. It tells the story without embellishment. It is brief and to the

point. This is how the modest, twenty-eight year old sergeant from Keith in Banffshire would have wished it and in a way, even for him, it would have been too much, too fulsome in describing his part in the incident.

A fortnight later during the Battle of the Odon in a letter to his brother George he wrote:

"Behind us lies the bitterest fighting I have ever experienced. As we expected we got a pretty important role and although there were times when we felt it was going to be too much for us the knowledge that

Top left: HM The Queen inspects men of the Black Watch just before the Normandy invasion in June 1944. In the background, Colonel J A Hopwood, General Sir Arthur Wauchope (Colonel of the Regiment) and Brigadier Oliver.

Bottom left: Preparing for the Normandy Landings. General Montgomery inspecting the Division's pipe band accompanied by Brigadier James Oliver DSO of the Black Watch.

Above: Transport of the Division being loaded aboard Liberty ships at East India Docks. June 3, 1944.

Battalion required immediate action and recognising the urgency I decided to put my own plan into operation without consulting an officer.

"Coupled with the speed and fanatical fighting which only desperation can prompt we laid the foundations for a decisive victory when by all the rules of military tactics we should have been beaten. As I was the senior rank present at the initial stages I got all the congratulations.

"The last straw came when the newsreel camera folk wanted a rehearsal for a 'take', so I said 'On your way, brother, the war's still on out here.''

For Willie McPherson, in common with most of his comrades, the war had been 'on' for far too long. His letters are threaded with a vein of weariness about the whole, depressing business, but despite the hardships and the setbacks there is never a grain of self-pity. In many instances, in both good and bad times, his perceptive comments, often serious, at times humorous, must have acted as a source of encouragement for those of his family who waited at home and wondered, like him, just how much longer the waiting and the wondering would have to be endured.

Willie McPherson was the youngest member of a family of twelve. His mother died when he was three weeks old and the responsibility of housekeeping for the family fell on the shoulders of his sixteen year old sister, Peggy. As a youngster he was diligent and industrious at school and such was his love of the outdoors that in his teenage and later years he spent most weekends cycling around the Scottish countryside, a haversack on his back containing a tent and primus stove. Until his conscription papers arrived he worked in a woollen mill in his home town and after joining the 5/7th Gordon Highlanders found himself in the Western Desert in August, 1942. He took part in the Battle of El Alamein and the rest of the campaign in North Africa and in May, 1943, before the Division commenced training for the invasion of Sicily was writing to his sister Peggy, to say:

"You will have heard long by this time hostilities out here are over and I know you will be waiting anxiously for the news that I have been favoured until the last and that I have escaped being wounded. At the cessation of hostilities I immediately sent off a cable so that you would know but three days later I got it back saying cables to the UK were cancelled.

"I am also sorry that I haven't been able

defeat would be disastrous kept us going. You will soon get the official story in the papers. You will read of a really terrific battle in which the Gordons once again emerged victorious to cover themselves with glory. Incidentally, if you read any story giving my name take it with a pinch of salt.

"I was interviewed by the observer officer and asked to describe the battle as I saw it but apart from saying 'We won' I had nothing to say. After he had gone the *Daily Express* war correspondent wanted an eye-witness account for broadcasting, but I said there were plenty of other men better fitted to tell the story then me, so the Padre gave the story and again stuck in my name. Actually, I'm afraid to think what the paper men will put in. You say one word and they make it a hundred and if it wasn't for the names of places, when reading it you would never recognise the incident.

"Whatever you read purporting to have been said by me or any description of what I did, disbelieve it. I dogmatically refused to say anything apart from two simple words, 'We won'. The credit really belongs to the boys without whose fine response there would have been a rather different story to tell. The throwing back of Jerry from the nerve centre of the to write sooner but Tunis had not been long taken when we turned our backs on the battlefield and have been travelling ever since. A memory of the rapid but wearying journeys after Aghelia, but this time there was not the hidden fear that the next bit of hidden ground would contain death or destruction and I write for the first time knowing that the silence and absence of shells and guns are indeed a real peace and not, as so often was the case, a calm before the storm.

"I know also you will be asking if we are coming home now that the fighting is over. I will not say or even attempt to guess but I will ask you to remember that even though the 51st played prominent parts in the 8th Army successes, it is nevertheless the 'youngest' member of a veteran 8th Army that careered several times up and down the desert, advancing, withdrawing, advancing, and getting no rest. Many of them have been in the desert since the war broke out. I do not say, however, we are not going home, in fact I think we have a fifty-fifty chance but in many ways I prefer having the whole show finished before I step ashore in Blighty again. But time will tell.

"We have been lucky. Never at any time were we faced with the prospect of defeat, thus we had amazing confidence in ourselves. Not for a minute will I suggest that the 51st fought better than any other unit, but the reputation and the fact that the 51st was in the line seemed to give the flanking units more confidence and confidence, believe it or not, wins the battles alone. Let us hope that having got on the road to victory we will know no halts."

A few days later Sgt McPherson was telling his brother, George:

"I still have no idea whether we shall go home or not, but with hostilities finished I could stay here long enough. The climate is not just unlike at home while it would be very easy to imagine you were in Scotland. The same green fields and trees, the same old hay making and ploughing and the same old hills. In fact I can very nearly claim to have travelled the length and breadth of Scotland and never have I seen such rocky mountain scenery during the four days travel to get here.

"You will be puzzling very much as to where I am, I know, but in the interests of security I cannot mention names. All the same I'm sure an intelligent guess will not be far wrong. Study the map and follow the line of our advance from Alamein – Tobruk – Benghazi – Tripoli – Sfax – Sousse – and Tunis . . !"*

It was November before the 5/7th Gordon Highlanders returned to the UK after the successful campaign in Sicily. Sgt McPherson found himself in various roles, but after the excitement of the previous year he was finding being back rather boring and restrictive mainly because he was stationed in the South of England at Chalfont St. Giles in Buckinghamshire many miles from his native North-East of Scotland. But his sense of humour was still present as illustrated by this event in February 1944:

"The pipes and drums of the Division are broadcasting on the 16th of this month but I don't know on what wavelength. And speaking about broadcasts there were two old geysers going round asking for criticisms of the Forces programme to the Middle East. They seemed more than a little surprised and, I suspect unbelieving, when I replied I wasn't in a position to criticise as I had never heard them. However, to be every bit as pointed in my answers as they were with their questions I told them if it was helpful advice they wanted I would suggest they looked around until they found someone from the base. The implied meaning did not however sink in and they had to ask where they would find 'someone from the base!' My reply was, 'Maybe still in Cairo' which prompted them to do the only polite thing they did – lift their hats and say 'Good Morning!'"

By March, 1944 Willie McPherson found himself being given the responsibility of

The landing at Berniéres-sur-Mer. REME troops of the Highland Division reading the booklet on France issued to them before embarkation. June 6, 1944.

*Sgt McPherson was at Djidjelli in Algeria.

training a reserve reconnaissance and harbour group. Obviously, although he was not aware of it at the time, the intensive training now getting underway was in preparation for the Allied invasion of Europe three months later. On March 12, after having been told by his Commanding Officer that "we should be prepared for something unexpected happening", he wrote:

"It is only five men and it mostly entails map reading and movement by compass. I'm not bothering too much about the compass training because it entails too much cross-country hiking at a time when bed is a better place. However, the map reading suits me down to the ground. We just get the bikes and I plot the route and say to one of them, 'Right, take me there'. We always do about sixty miles a day and we always draw up rations in case we get lost. We don't always get to the place I ordered but as I say they learn by their mistakes and it wouldn't give them any real experience if I told them when they were on the wrong roads. I merely make a note of the place and mistake and then point it out when we get back.

"Yesterday I laid out a route which should have taken us on the outskirts of Greater London, so when I saw we were actually in London itself I says, 'Right, we'll call it a day'. And the map reading exercise turned into a Saturday afternoon in London.

"The boys are fine pleased with themselves and think its a great job, but they have a shock coming to them. After they are past the initial stage they come off the road and get on to the ground work which has mostly to be done on foot. I give them a series of map references, they go there and find the next map reference from there – something like a treasure hunt. So, I daresay when they get down to the more serious side of it they will get a bit fed up. However, as I warned them, it was easy enough here when they knew there was nobody waiting or looking for them and they were always sure of their breakfast.

"By the way, the CO wanted to send me off on a three weeks course learning to speak German. If it had been in the Army's time I would have gone but it was to take two hours every evening for four nights a week. Anyway, when a thing is sort of voluntary I'm always dubious about it and it would mostly be learning German military vocabulary and wouldn't be of much use. So I had to talk myself out of that little lot, leaving the old colonel thinking I wasn't just the man for the job."

Scenes on the way across to Normandy. June 6, 1944.

On D-Day, June 6, 1944 Sgt McPherson was at the forefront of the action as the Allied forces made their assault on Europe. The 5/7th Gordon Highlanders was the first battalion of the Highland Division to set foot on French soil. On June 14, two days after the events for which he was awarded the Military Medal he was writing home to say:

"I'm still very much fit and well. They are still very careful as regards where we are or what we're doing, but in keeping with our reputation "Ask and it is done" still broadly covers our entire situation. We are now in a position not only to hold all comers, but to throw out the challenge to Jerry to fight when and where we like. The object of our campaign can, I think, be quite clear – to knock the Nazis out of this war. I still cannot say in what period we hope to do it but at this stage nothing has happened to make us think any different."

On June 26 Willie McPherson was still remarkably cheerful despite the fierce and intensive fighting he had just experienced.

"Things have quietened down considerably with us. They have opened rest camps here already, so many chaps going each day for a number of days. I was down to go today but I said, 'I'll wait for a bit to see if I don't get mine in Blighty'. That's how well the war is going for us now."

A week later, following publication in a newspaper of a photograph showing Sgt McPherson guarding some prisoners, he wrote to his brother, George, to say:

"It rather shook me to hear I was photographed taking in three prisoners. I never noticed the cameramen at all. Incidentally, those three were really lucky I took them instead of shooting. Just five minutes before that I saw two of our stretcher-bearers killed by a Jerry machine-gun post from about twenty-five yards range. They were murdered in cold blood because they were not carrying weapons of any description and were wearing the Red-Cross armbands which could not have been mistaken at that range. In any case they had their stretcher and were picking up the wounded. I swore there and then I would never take another prisoner.

"The three in question were rendered bomb-happy by a few hand grenades thrown in the ditch and the sorry state they came in, hands up and 'Kamerading' at some tune, beat me. My finger itched to pull the trigger, but it would have been too much like murder. I felt I had to work off my temper somehow though and I took them over to see the dead stretcher-bearers still lying clutching the stretcher, told them I was going to murder them just as my friends had been – shot unarmed. To lend some truth to my story I had them dig and they then broke down. They didn't know they were digging temporary graves for the British and German dead. However, I felt the longer I kept them the more tempted I would be to shoot so I had them sent back to Brigade for interrogation.

"The British intelligence officer later told me that they reached Brigade in a state of absolute funk and they supplied a mine of information which made them more valuable alive after all."

Shortly afterwards Willie McPherson's sense of humour had returned.
"In the first month's fighting I have but one regret – my cap badge (the one Betty sent to Africa) is now, I fear, a battle trophy for some lousy Nazi. While reccying a route which should have been in our hands a sniper whipped my cap off while I was cruising merrily along on the bike. Experts will tell you an army motor bike's limit is 65mph. I could tell them something different now. From a safe range I cursed and fumed and looking longingly along the road actually saw the blighter come out and pick up my cap. I cursed him, I cursed the war, I cursed my sten gun because I knew he was out of range; what angered me even more I knew he was probably equipped with a proper sniper's rifle in which I was, in all probability, still in range. So, the most awkward I could make myself was to hope the bullet struck the badge and broke it, or better still that he never found it. As I've often been told, I may, after all, have a charmed life."

In a further letter Sgt McPherson wrote in praise of the section of men which he led.
"I may be boasting, but I'm proud of the fact that I've never sent a man where I was afraid to go myself. I am tremendously proud of my section. I'm perhaps a trifle hard on them at times, because even in comparative safety I insist on digging in, often they being the only ones having to do so, but the fact that I've never lost any of my section due to enemy action does, I think, speak for itself. All the same, if at times I appear as a hard taskmaster it has, assisted by the grace of God, paid a rich dividend. Yes, they have got more kicks than pats, but secretly I think the world of them and if anything happened to any of them I'd hate to think how it would shake me. I only hope that each and every one of them come smiling through."

Three days later:

"My spirits have been dampened considerably by the events of the past few days. First, we lost the CO* with a head injury by shell. The newcomer is the sixth commanding officer I will have served under in the field. First impressions are not very good. Within the first hour of his arrival he was laying down his routine. Wash and shave, boots brushed every morning. I wonder if a man dies happier when he's newly washed, or his boots are clean. These orders we accepted with the silent contempt they deserve. Maybe in a few day's time he will experience for himself what we have experienced many times in the past – that is, no time or water to cook meals each morning far less wash and shave. We would have liked to have had him in the desert where we scorned carrying an extra postage stamp far less a boot brush. His coming has renewed an oft-times thought and desire to shake off a responsibility I have often felt was too much for me. The plain truth is we've been at it too long. We've been asked to do too much.

"Today we lost the Doc – killed by a 'Moaning Minnie'. That was a bitter blow. He had come all the way from Alamein with us and his steady courage, and almost inexhaustible physical endurance I had a great admiration for. My job entails me knowing every position in the Battalion and after any heavy shelling the Doc was always out around the positions looking for the wounded rather than wait till they were brought in. To save time, others duties permitting, I invariably accompanied him, which act being in no way obligatory he always appreciated. From his cold courage I have

*Lt Col. J. E. G. Hay.

often drawn the inspiration and ability to carry on. I will miss him and so will the Battalion for I cannot recollect a time when he was not on the spot when wanted.

"A direct hit on his trench killed him in his sleep. A poor finish to such an active man. Strange, I never visualised the Doc getting it."

For a week Sgt McPherson was able to relax away from the front line and the sound of battle and managed to write:

"I now feel ever so much fitter both in mind and body. It's strange that a few days absent from the sound of shot and shell is sufficient to make one forget so much. But perhaps it's just as well.

"I toured pretty extensively on the motor-bike and couldn't help thinking what a fine holiday could have been spent in France with the bike and the primus. In the midst of my travels I made a point of visiting the British military cemetery at Hermanville. The cemetery lies in a quiet little orchard, gently swept by the cool breeze from the sea, a cool glade shaded from the sun by the trees. It is well cared for and while there I watched a French family reverently place some flowers at the foot of the neat, plain little crosses. The man and wife with their two little girls walked close by me. I asked – did they know any of these dead heroes to whom they brought flowers? No, they said. It was but a silent appreciation of the men who gave so much in the liberation of their country.

"I pointed out the grave of a friend of mine, told them I had come to see it and they told me his grave would never lack a fresh flower so long as they were in the district. So I thanked them and left them, meditating on just why the French people take so easily to the ravages of war. No matter how much they have lost they just

Scenes on the way across the English Channel, June 6, 1944.

shrug their shoulders and murmur 'C'est le guerre' (This is war)."

On August 9 Sgt McPherson was slightly wounded but according to the official notification sent to his father, "remained on duty in North-West Europe." Around this time he wrote one of his longest and most comprehensive accounts of the campaign and explained to his family for the first time the exact nature of the action that had won him the Military Medal.

"Just as it broke daylight we were dealt a surprise attack by an enemy group about thirty strong. He succeeded in jockeying position and with a Spandau machine gun swept the ground keeping us down. Temporarily lost, I managed to get up against a low dyke and by playing my sten-gun fire forced the gunners back into the orchard. The hand grenade I threw did no more damage than force them out of the fox-hole while the Germans' excited shout for 'hand grenades' warned me to lie low and I was saved by the dyke. Another burst from my sten-gun and opposition from enemy fire ceased.

"I seized this opportunity to get organised and got the boys lined behind the dyke. In later days it became spoken of as 'the thin red line'. Lying low for a few minutes we kept a silent watch and managed to spot a few of the Nazis behind and up trees. So I called for a small arms barrage to cover the whole orchard. Everything we had we threw in for ten minutes and during those ten minutes from volunteers I organised a forward sweep as soon as our fire ceased.

"The Nazis, broken and dazed by the intensity of our fire, were forced to break formation and our forward sweep claimed nine dead, three prisoners, one wounded, while we had the satisfaction of seeing the remaining twenty odd fleeing back to their own lines, many of them disarmed. Including the bodies we captured four Spandau machine guns and two sniper's rifles. It was a good morning's work. The best tribute to its success, however, was the CO's orders at a subsequent attack to line the same wall and from there we held all comers from one o'clock in the morning until daylight. The CO's decision to make this wall the mainstay of our defence I gloried in, as an unwitting verification of my own sound judgement in deciding to stand there in the first place.

"We perhaps haven't made the same headlines in the papers as the Americans taking Cherbourg, but for sheer hard slogging we have taken the heaviest of the fighting. There are many stories of un-

believable bravery. A Sgt Fraser and his gun crew took all honours for saving the day on another occasion. The German tanks had broken through. They were only about three hundred yards from us. I prepared myself for the POW camp by throwing away any souvenirs which would have connected me with their unfortunate Nazi comrades of previous attacks, in addition to my own army watch so they couldn't rifle me of anything valuable, pulled up a further supply of ammo and prepared to fight it out.

"Fraser gave the order to fire and the leading tank went up in flames. Nice work, Jack – a real brew up. A second tank, however, swings round past the first one, its guns trained on our guns vainly trying to knock it out. I begin to feel downhearted now – this second tank still advancing. Five hundred -400 -300 -200, By God Jack you don't know how I've been sweating, but there's another lovely brew. From out of the black smoke there emerges another advancing vehicle, an armoured car. 'Stand by, lads!'. Load – Range –On Target –FIRE!' And the last threat for this attack is over. But that gun crew – heroes all.

"And we have Sgt Stephen. His individual lone patrols brings him fourteen enemy snipers to his credit. We have Sgt Aitkenhead. Taken prisoner he overcame his escort, killed them and reported back in his own lines for duty. Still another sergeant – Sgt Gardiner – accompanied by

A vehicle is prepared for the landing. Behind the man with outstretched arm can be seen the hole in the side of the ship made by a beach mine.

Coming ashore with dry feet – this time in Normandy. June, 1944. There is an HD sign on the truck. The guns in the foreground are Bofors.

Pte McLure from Skye. They were cut off and surrounded, but together with a bren gun they shot, hid, crawled and manoeuvred their way back to the Battalion again.

"Perhaps the greatness of our task was our inspiration. We were the people who had been brought together to make the initial European invasion. On us depended whether or not Allied forces would remain in Europe. The appeal to fight to the last was needless. We were here and here we would – and will – stay. To no-one could the news of Cherbourg's capture have sounded better than to us. Here were the fruits of our labours. The vital period has passed. Every day we increase our grip on the Continent.

"Montgomery is jubilant while we have that strange satisfaction that only victory, when defeat seemed inevitable, can give you. During these long weary days and nights you may ask what was my greatest wish. I'll tell you. A peaceful sleep, a sleep which didn't mean one eye open or the jumping awake expecting to see a German standing over you – to get the boots and trousers off – any of those things in these desperate days would have been Heaven.

"And that was our contribution to the opening of the invasion. I do not suggest that even now we are finished, but now as at Alamein I said, 'The worst is past'. So do I believe that no matter what role we may figure in in future operations the same desperate back-to-the-wall bitter

fighting for breathing space cannot be relived. And if I'm proud of the Regiment, Brigade or Division, can you blame me? They gave so much. They did so much and through it all I have borne a charmed life.

"The boys marvel at my apparent lack of nerve. Some say 'He'll get it yet'. Others refer to me as mad, while I myself – well, if they only knew how really scared I am, how I've had to fight it, how I've had to bluff it, to carry on to be able to say, 'I've not let them down'. Frankly, every day that passes I feel less able to meet the responsibilities thrown on me, but with boys like I've just told you about I just cannot let them down. If they can stick it – I can stick it. But how, oh how, I would welcome the finish of it all.

"These are my experiences. You may think I'm losing heart. I'm not, but I admit I'm beginning to feel war-weary in common with the rest of the old hands. We've done so much to win this war, so much to be proud of, I'd hate to think we couldn't last it out now".

On August 29, 1944 Willie McPherson was killed in action. On a steep winding road running through a wood overlooking the River Seine a Spandau machine-gun opened up on the patrol he was leading. He died instantly. The men he had led so successfully through innumerable difficult and dangerous times escaped unscathed.

105

At Colombelles and Goch

Gordon Highlanders moving
forward in heavy rain,
Normandy, June 1944.

The gun crew of an HD six pounder anti-tank gun. Left to right:- L/Sergeant J Fraser of Lesmahagow, Scotland; Private J Fagan of Kilmarnock; Private Franks of London and Private D Pitt of Glasgow, of the 5th/7th Gordons, in the Bois-de-Bevent area, June 17, 1944.

Up to July, 1944, Lt Col Alexander Brodie saw, in his own words, 'little active service'. He had served in Palestine and been a liaison officer with the Polish Carpathian Brigade Group in Torbruk during the siege in 1941. After a spell with the 2nd Battalion The Black Watch in Syria in January, 1942 he was sent to India. Returning to the UK in January, 1944 he was posted to the 4th (City of Dundee) Bn The Black Watch. In June of that year the three Black Watch Battalions in the 51st Highland Division, the 1st, 5th (County of Angus) and the 7th (County of Fife) suffered heavy casualties in Normandy and asked for junior officers and NCO's to be sent out from the Black Watch battalions at home.

Individual officers had been requested by name and as Brodie was to learn later, his name was not included. However, Berewold Innes, his commanding officer at the time, knew he was eager to do 'some real fighting' as he called it, and sent him along with the others.

In all Brodie was to spend no more than three periods of about six to eight weeks with the Highland Division during which time "I would be wounded not too seriously, have a good time at home as a wounded hero and return fresh to rejoin my braver and tougher friends. Most of the officers in the 51st Division had a worse time than me – and for much longer".

However, despite his reticence there are many soldiers from various units and battalions within the Division who remember his name and much to his dismay various stories of his exploits have been embroidered in the telling over the years since the war. But despite events there is little doubt that his sense of humour, a love of the ridiculous, a healthy disregard for misplaced authority, earned him the respect of the majority who served under him. When he set off for Normandy he held the substantive rank of Captain.

"Because of this I was senior to most of the Territorial Majors and, of course, no commanding officer wished to reduce any of these to fit me in. After all, they had all seen more action than me and had proved themselves. I did not worry about this, for I knew they deserved their rank and I had not earned it. I could easily have found a Major's appointment if I had been prepared to stay at home.

So, at the end of June, I accompanied a small draft of junior officers and NCO's under Major Graham Pilcher, a popular Territorial Major of the 4th Bn who had been very nice to me when I arrived in January. We eventually arrived at Ranville, where we joined the Fifth Bn. It had suffered badly at Bréville a few days before and had received drafts from two English infantry regiments.

Men of the 5th/7th Gordon Highlanders brew up round a slit trench in the woods near Touffreville, Normandy. June 17, 1944.

Lt Col C. N. Thomson, a very famous Territorial Officer, greeted Graham Pilcher warmly, but contrived to conceal his delight at getting me. He led Graham into the orchard and, so I believe, asked what I was like. Graham gave me a good character, and I was then led into the orchard. "As you are here, you may stay for the time being. But, I should make it quite clear, this is a Territorial Battalion and we don't like Regular Officers."

I then took over 'A' Coy. This had lost all its officers and most of its NCO's and men at Bréville in early June. The Company Commander, Major John MacGregor, was a much loved and very competent officer. He had been very badly wounded. He recovered, and, after the war he commanded the London Scottish. He was not an easy person to succeed.

'A' Coy now consisted of very young Cockneys from an English Régiment. They were, I think, rather overawed at being in the Black Watch, and expected it would be far too exciting for them. The Sgt Major was a Regular, who had been a signaller. I did not remember him, but he knew me all right. The CQMS was Meekison, a Territorial who eventually became RQMS. He was absolutely excellent as, so I found were all the CQMS's in the Fifth Bn. The Company second in Command was Bill Johnstone. He was a Glaswegian, and had been a Sergeant in the Territorials in 1939. He had been

through the Desert and Sicily with the Battalion.

All the officers except Bill Johnstone, were a little older than me, and I was 32 two weeks later. They had all come into the Company, and, in the case of the platoon commanders, the Bn, since Bréville, and had seen as little active service as me. But they were all thoroughly decent, and with such young soldiers, I was probably lucky to have officers of mature age. Dashing young subalterns would have scared the soldiers. The NCO's, too, were inexperienced and had arrived since Bréville. The few soldiers who had survived Bréville were no help. They had been thoroughly frightened and had lost their friends. If I had been more experienced, I would have had them posted, but I was still feeling my way, so I lacked the confidence to ask for this to be done.

We spent a few days at Ranville, bivouaced in an orchard. The young soldiers were cheerful and I did my best to get to know them, and let them know me. Soon, we were told to take over Ste Honorine la Chardonerette from the Fifth (Caithness and Sutherland) Bn The Seaforth Highlanders and I went forward with the other company commanders to see the positions we were to occupy. We passed a huge meadow where the gliders and parachutes had landed on D Day, and the silk parachutes came in handy for covering weapons and protecting them from dust. I asked what the etiquette was if we heard a shell coming over as we walked up the road. Did we stoically walk on or jump into the ditch? Being new, I did not want to do the wrong thing. But I got no reply, not even a derisive one.

The Fifth Seaforth seemed to have had a bad time. A German patrol had come right up to them and thrown grenades into a section and there had been some shelling. They seemed very worried about showing lights in buildings they occupied but had done nothing to block the windows, and they seemed to have easy-going habits as regards sentries in the forward platoons. The actual relief went well. Relief in the line had never been practised in peacetime, so I had no experience of it. Various stores and weapons – I remember there were some American machine-guns – had to be taken over, and the positions of neighbouring posts and mines and what was known of the enemy all had to be passed to the relieving unit in whispers and in the dark. The outgoing unit was only too anxious to be off, and the incomers left bewildered and a little apprehensive.

A company of the Gordons was under command of the Battalion in Ste Honorine, and next day, the Company Commander came to see me. He warned me that his men fired first and challenged afterwards so would we keep clear of his position at night. I replied that we used cold steel, and his men would be perfectly safe with us. He asked if he could keep his company jeep in my HQ and I agreed. The thing turned up full of ammunition and flying a Red Cross flag. I made a fuss, and either the Red Cross flag or the ammunition was removed. I forget now. But it caused some surprise at the time. I considered that if this jeep fell into enemy hands, they would be justified in shooting any of us they caught.

One night, a patrol from another company discovered or, rather heard, a German working party about a mile in front of us. I was told to take out a fighting patrol the next night to snatch a prisoner. I was given very strict orders that I personally was not to take part in the actual snatch, which would be carried out by David Law, one of the subalterns and two or three men he had chosen. I was to lead the patrol to a place close to where the German working party was supposed to be, and bring it and the captives home again. I was elaborately briefed as to where the Germans were meant to be, with a map and an air photo. But the trouble was that no-one was really quite sure. The patrol which had reported them were shaken and exhausted by the strain of their activities and it was clearly useless to ask for one of them as a guide. It would also have made a poor impression to suggest that the Germans would not necessarily be working in the same place. I suspected that the whole idea was really to test my nerve. Having done a good deal of night patrolling in Palestine in 1938, this sort of thing did not worry me, but I did not expect anyone to believe this. In any case patrolling against not at all heroic Palestine Arabs was not the same as patrolling against the more pugnacious Germans.

We spent the day rehearsing moves and signals and prepared the arms and equipment we were to take. I forget the details, but David Law said he did not need to take a weapon. His strong arms and knobby fists were enough. As far as I remember we took sten guns, phosphorous grenades and bayonets and some sort of club – pick helves or entrenching tool handles I expect.

I told the men to take all the rest they could, and they managed to have quite a lot. I found myself involved in all sorts of administration. Bill Johnstone did most of it, but, of course, on this day of days, there had to be problems with which only I could deal. However, at about 8pm shortly before dark, I lay down and dropped off to be awoken because the gunners who were to cover our withdrawal with our prisoners, were now going to register the area and perhaps I should watch so that I was quite sure where I was expected to go. I said either I was to be allowed to sleep, or the patrol must be put off for two hours so that I could sleep after the artillery registration and that I did not recommend such a postponement as it would add to the tension the men were having to put up with. So I was left alone and had a much needed zizz.

We duly set off and crept slowly to what I thought was to be our jump-off place for the snatch. Not a sound nor anything to be seen and it was not a very dark night. David and his thugs crept away, but found nothing, so we started home. We moved a good deal faster than we had moved out and I suppose the Germans heard us, for a machine-gun began firing from nowhere near where we expected the enemy to be. It did no harm and we arrived back without incident. Approaching our own people from the direction of the enemy was fairly exciting. Luckily, the company through which we passed was alert but not trigger happy. Indeed, it was overconfident, and I had to warn them to check us in carefully in case the enemy were trying to slip in on our heels. The young soldiers had behaved well and had every reason to swagger a bit, for patrolling in front of our own lines was potentially dangerous, and, during their training, the dangers had been perhaps too well explained. So the very word patrol could send shivers down people's backs as I learned later on.

About July 9, 1944, we were relieved by the Gordons to take part in the attack on Colombelles Factory. We marched out to some fields near Ranville, where we dug in and rested. July 10 was my 32nd birthday and in a neighbouring farm house we got our orders for the attack.

The point was that Caen had fallen a few days before, and supply convoys going to Caen were being accurately shelled. The Germans were thought to have occupied the tall brick chimneys of the metallurgic factory at Colombelles. How they got up the chimneys was never discussed, but the factory stood on high ground and no doubt did provide good observation. A battalion of the Gordons was to move up the Orne Canal and the Fifth Battalion, meaning us, was to move

across the open ground on their left or Eastern flank. The attack was to take place at night. It was considered to be unsound and our orders were delayed while the Commanding Officer, Lt Col C. N. "Chick" Thomson, and Brigadier Murray went to see the GOC of the Division to have the thing cancelled, but they failed. We were to have enormous artillery support, the place was to be bombed by the RAF and there were to be ten tanks supporting the Fifth Battalion. (I only saw one in the dawn's early light, and it was going the wrong way very much faster than I thought a tank could move.)

However, I went back to 'A' Company and gave them their orders. Just before, I went back to Ste Honorine, from where I could get a look at the ground over which we were to go. I was to take the Company half way to the factory and occupy a 'firm base', as the term was, along a sunken lane running across the front with a farm

Top left: A patrol of the Division moving cautiously through the woods in the Bois-de-Bevant area searching for snipers. June 1944.

Bottom left: Scouts from a patrol of the 5th/7th Gordons watch for enemy movements beyond the woods in the Bois-de-Bevant area. June 17, 1944.

Top: A company of Gordons holding a position in the Touffreville sector leave their slit trenches to smile at the official photographer. June 17th, 1944.

Above left: A Gordon's Bren carrier loaded with ammunition, ablaze after being hit by German machine gun fire, near Touffreville. June 1944.

steading on the right and a cottage surrounded by a stone wall on the left, where a road ran from the factory towards Ste Honorine and crossed the sunken lane. The rest of the Battalion were to go on to the factory, chase out the Germans, and cover the Sappers, while they blew down the chimneys. Then everyone was to go home to tea.

I duly briefed the Company about what was to happen and then addressed them. I was only too well aware that the Division had surrendered in 1940, and there was a tendency to make out that this was a heroic act. Not having been there, I cannot comment, but I believed that the surrender of this very famous division had made much of the rest of the Army believe that it was not too bad a thing to pack it in. Somehow, the newspapers had given the impression that to throw oneself on the mercy of the enemy was nothing to be ashamed of. I did realise that it would be very difficult to allow my men to be killed when, by surrendering, I could save their lives. So I told them that, while I would not hesitate to shoot any one who ran away, I expected them to shoot me or any officer or NCO who ordered them to pack in. To my surprise, this rather frightened them, and, soon after, Bill Johnstone told me that our two stretcher bearers had disappeared. These had both been at Bréville, and no doubt their courage had been worn away. Two more were provided by the Battalion HQ. These turned out to be very stout fellows. I do not know what happened to the two runaways.

It is perhaps worth discussing the problem of cowards in war time. By making off before or during a battle, men add to the difficulties and dangers of those they leave behind. They may have to carry extra loads of ammunition and stores, and will certainly get less sleep during operations, because their turn to be sentries will come round more frequently. I found weariness and lack of sleep the worst of the strains of war. The establishment of a rifle company was about 110, of which about 15 were cooks, drivers and storemen, so the company should have had about 95 to go into action. In fact, companies were very lucky if they numbered 60, all ranks. So anyone running away caused bitter feelings.

Many of us thought the death penalty should have been restored. But then, who was to pass such a sentence on anyone? Officers from the infantry could hardly be spared to sit on the necessary court martial, so the runaways would be tried by officers who did not have to face the same dangers as the infantry. Artillery or

Service Corps or Engineers or Gunner officers certainly shared the dangers of the infantry companies, but they always went back at night to their batteries where they got rather more sleep than the infantry Officers. Indeed, when they came back next morning, they did what they could to take some of the burden off the infantry officers over and above their specialist duties so that they could get some sleep. But all of these officers said they really could not be expected to condemn a soldier to death for failing to face dangers that they themselves never had to face. In the Great War, officers of all Services seem to have been much tougher in this respect than we were, but they did not like it.

Of course, a man who is at the end of his tether ought to be sent back before he disgraces himself, but, usually, he just could not be spared. He might have lain squealing in the bottom of a trench when the enemy attacked, but at least his comrades had the use of the ammunition he carried and he could do his turn as a sentry, admittedly an unreliable one, at night. Before I went into action, I used to be horrified at the idea of a tired frightened man being shot by his comrades and I hoped I should never have to be present at such a performance. But when I saw the extra strain and fatigue such men imposed on the rest, I thought differently.

On the night of July 10/11 we set off for the forming-up place. The English regiment from which most of 'A' Coy came, had been the demonstration battalion at the School of Infantry, then at Barnard Castle, and used to give a spectacular demonstration of forming-up for a night attack, so I thought all would be well. So I set off rather early, making the men move along the grass verges on each side of the road and having ensured that their accoutrements would not rattle.

Top left: A German prisoner brought in by one of the patrols is searched by Captain J Stuart-Black of 'C' Company, 5th/7th Gordon Highlanders. June 1944.

Bottom left: Major General Bullen-Smith commander of the Highland Division and Brigadier Murray of 153rd Brigade photographed at the Brigade's TAC Headquarters.

Below: An officer of the Division, taking particulars from a German prisoner outside Longueval.

We then halted astride the road, about 150 yards from the forming-up place, all carefully taped out by the Battalion Pioneers. Then there was a mighty clatter along the road and the tramp tramp of marching feet, and right along the middle of the road, fair-filleting 'A' Coy sitting on each side of the road, came 'B' Coy and Graham Pilcher. I was rather shocked but had to laugh. We managed to sort things out without too much noise.

Then came the moment to form-up. 'A' Company was the leading company, and I marched them to our tapes. School of Infantry or no School of Infantry, there was chaos as sections got mixed up and individuals went astray. However, it was sorted out reasonably quietly, and then one of the platoon commanders asked me when the men were to load. It had not occurred to me that they were not loaded, but I had given no orders covering this, and so I was entirely to blame. The darkness hid my shame.

'A' Coy's objective was at an angle to the forward edge of the forming-up place, which was parallel to the edge of Colombelles factory which the rest of the Fifth Bn were to capture. So I decided to start a minute before H-hr, when the artillery would begin to fire, because I had learned from a demonstration at the School of Infantry what a row the guns made and knew I would never be able to make the slight change of direction necessary once they started to fire. I think I had explained this to the platoon commanders because it worked and somehow we had the unwieldy mass moving in the right direction just as the artillery started. I yelled encouragement, but, as I could not myself hear what I was saying, the men had to do without it.

We reached the sunken lane, and found that there was a wide grass verge on the enemy side of the lane, and then the bank. I told the men to dig in against the bank and to throw the excavated earth behind them. This they did not understand because, in their training, they had always been told to throw the earth in front to form a parapet. However, Bill Johnstone and the CSM managed to get Coy HQ to carry out this heretical order. All the same I found some of the platoons laboriously throwing the earth on top of the bank in front of them when I set off to visit them which I did as soon as Coy HQ was more or less settled down to digging. I told my servant, a rather nervous Cockney named Palmer to dig a specially big hole as I should be sharing it with him, and this rather shook him. He had been rather shaken two or three days before by

Captured German officers being marched in. June 25, 1944.

a shell bursting near him and I think he was in a daze, for I had warned him beforehand. I had realised that the men would be rather dazed by all the noise and their natural apprehension at their first attack, but I did not realise how much it would affect their behaviour. Bill Johnstone and his servant, an Aberdonian, Macleod, had been through all this before and were perfectly calm and this steadied the men in Coy HQ.

Then along came Charles Munro, OC 'C' Coy, and his Coy HQ. He asked me if I had seen his company which he had lost. As I remember, this Company was to halt at the edge of the factory and the other two were to go in and clear out the Germans. I expect that he had lost control owing to the din of the artillery fire. I could only tell where they were not and he vanished into the darkness. He was wounded three days later, and was killed at Antwerp by a flying bomb in November '44. But what happened to him and his company at Colombelles, I have forgotten.

Later, a few Germans came in with their hands up. They told me they were Poles compelled to serve with the Germans and that they had surrendered as soon as they safely could. One even asked to go back and fetch one of his friends who hadn't managed it yet. But I checked them for arms and sent them on back. The Germans were good at making young men from conquered countries fight for them. They hardly ever deserted until our own troops or the Americans came right up to them.

Next, George Dunn, the second-in-command of the Battalion came along

114

and the Germans began firing mortars at us. They burst like a Bengal fountain and I, new to it all, remarked how pretty they looked. George drily said "From a distance" and off he went forward.

Then two signallers from Bn HQ, who had been laying a telephone wire, fell into one of our slit trenches. They had been caught by a flurry of artillery or mortar fire near the cottage by the crossroads and were pretty scared. But they reported one of my men wounded there, so I told the company carrier and the two stretcher bearers we would go and fetch him. The driver said "Are you coming too?" and I said "Of course" and he said "Good show", which of course, it was not. I should have stayed with my HQ and, possibly, sent Bill Johnstone or the CSM, if anyone at all but I did know the way and perhaps I was trying to build a legend.

Anyway, off we went and all we found was a trooper from the Tanks with a wounded hand and pretty shocked. We gave him a drink of water and pointed him in the right direction. He thanked us and went off. We returned to the Coy HQ and I told the signallers that they were wrong and there was only this tankateer there. But one of them, Brunton, said "You must have missed him", and, very stoutly, for he was still a little shaken, said he would come with us and so off we went again. Sure enough, we found a poor little chap with both legs blown off above the knees, moaning softly and, I remember, he was saying 'Oh, dear! Oh dear!' The stretcher bearer shook his head and, I thought, looked pointedly at my revolver.

I think the soldier was not in pain. He was very young and surprisingly to me, there was no blood to be seen. It was getting light and he looked yellow. We lifted him on to the carrier, and away it went. Many drivers would have lingered at the Regimental Post, but this one hurried back to us as soon as he could. The signaller and I and the stretcher bearers started back. It was getting lighter, and the Germans must have seen what we were doing. The signaller had his rifle and I had picked up the casualty's rifle so we were an armed party. The Germans did not shoot till the carrier moved off; then they opened up on us. The German Army was pretty correct in these matters.

This distressing incident, to my surprise, did not affect me at all. I had thought I was more sensitive and would be very upset, but to my shame, the whole business left me quite unaffected. I suppose I was really preoccupied with my job, and so had no place in my mind or emotions to take in the horror and tragedy. I do know that, at the time, I was surprised to find how callous I was.

There was quite a lot of shooting and mortar fire at our lane. I heard the Coy Signaller talking over the No 18 wireless set to Bn, and he was saying "It is really awful here". I rebuked him and said it could be much worse and he really must not be so windy. He indignantly replied that he was talking about the wireless reception, so I said I was sorry, and, as he subsequently became the Bn HQ Signaller, it was just as well. I always found it paid to be polite to soldiers because, when things were shaky, my

Seaforths in extended order awaiting the order to advance, Normandy, June 1944.

115

oaths and more vigorous manners were more effective than if I had been cursing and swearing all the time.

I managed to get a compass bearing on an 88 gun that was firing at us, rather ineffectively. I do not think the Germans appreciated the wide verge to the lane and that we were therefore a bit closer to them than the lane itself, so they were firing a little high. One or two mortar bombs did land on the position and the CSM and my servant, poor Palmer, were badly shaken and I sent them to the RAP. Palmer said 'Good bye' and murmured he was sorry, he had not realised he had to dig my slit trench as well. In fact, I had dug most of it in the intervals of roaming around. The men were all well down in their slits, except Bill Johnstone and his man, Macleod, who were peering to the front all the time.

I started to write a message about the 88 gun, but all the business of getting the bearings and the map references correct bored me, so I decided to go off to the command post which I knew to be in a quarry or sand pit just behind my right hand platoon, which I could visit on the way. I could also find out just what had happened to the rest of the battalion for, although I could hear plenty of noise from the factory about three-quarters of a mile in front I had not intercepted any messages and was naturally interested. Again, I should have stayed with the Coy HQ and perhaps sent Bill Johnstone, but every one seemed reasonably cheerful, so off I went.

At the sand pit, all I found was a dead Gunner.

On the lip of the sand pit, I found the CSM and clerk and one or two others from the support company. They had all been wounded, but the CSM was keeping them cheerful. He was young, with dark hair, rosy cheeks, and horn rimmed spectacles. He was tall and strong looking. He had come out on the same draft as Graham Pilcher and me. I think he had been with the 10th Battalion. This little party was lying in a row, waiting for something to happen. They had all put on their field dressings and they were calm. I told them that I would send along the company carrier and they said 'Thank you very much'. Though, like all east of Scotland regiments, we could be pretty forthright with each other, all ranks in the Black Watch, Regular and Territorial, are polite. It took more than a first battle or a wound to spoil our manners. I returned to the Coy HQ and made the necessary arrangements.

About 0600hrs and now broad daylight

a scout car appeared with the adjutant, David MacIntyre. He told us that the attack had failed and the battalion would shortly retire through us under cover of smoke. I was to go when they were well clear. I forget the details. I sent out the runners to tell the platoons. One never arrived, and so David Law's platoon stayed out all day, captured a German patrol, and came home at supper time. But all this was after I was wounded.

Then, as an afterthought I decided to visit the battalion 6pdr anti-tank gun at the cottage by the cross roads, and tell them what to expect. When I arrived there, I found the gun but no crew. They had even left their bedding rolls behind. I sent a carrier along which hooked up the gun, looted the abandoned bedding rolls and took the gun back. I was rather shocked by the disappearance of the gun team, but I suppose they felt abandoned and lost. Had they been under my command, and not in support, I should myself have taken some interest in them, but, as it was, I did not bother about them, for I regarded them as a purely anti-tank platoon responsibility, which of course they were, but their officer was naturally far more preoccupied with the guns with the forward companies. I should have thought of all this at the time, but I did not.

This gun was recovered all right and I went back to Coy HQ and told them to load the jeep with the tools and blankets and all the other paraphernalia we had with us. By this time Coy HQ knew a withdrawal was taking place and I heard some one say 'He thinks the bloody blankets are more important than our copulating lives'. I said they were not, but that their honour and the Company's certainly were, and I was going to see that, if we had to go, we took everything with us. I cannot say this galvanised them, but everything was loaded on to the jeep; Bill went round the slit trenches to see that nothing was left behind. I sent them all off and Bill and Maclean and I went to visit the right hand platoon and the artillery 17 pdr. By this time, the smoke was coming down between us and the factory.

As we moved up the lane towards the right hand platoon, we met the artillery 17 pdr team. This was commanded by a lance-bombadier, and he had removed the sights and odd bits of his gun, and was obviously in some doubt as to whether he should have left. He was very young, but clearly more of a soldier than his officer. I told him we would get his gun out and asked him to come back to show us how to put the split trail together. This he did,

sending his team off with the gun sights and other bits he had removed. As I think over it all, I cannot imagine why I did not order the gun team back to cover the withdrawal of our forward coys from the factory. But what I did was never questioned, so I suppose I did more or less right. I cannot now remember exactly what my orders were. I do remember that I was perfectly calm and not the least frightened or in any doubt about what to do. In the whole action until I was wounded, my head was clear, and I was completely self confident, far more so than during an audit board or a general inspection.

Then the smoke lifted and I saw what turned out to be 'D' Coy moving back towards me, slowly, in perfect control. This was always a good company and its commander then was Major Joe Wright. He had been a great help to me during my brief stay with the Fifth Bn and was killed by a flying bomb at Antwerp with Charles Monro at the end of 1944. He was tall, dark, with a red face and a slightly ironic sense of humour.

At this time, Bill Johnstone and I and Macleod and a section of my right hand platoon were in a small farmyard. The artillery 17 pdr was pointing over the bank towards the enemy across the fields. It was partially dug in and quite difficult to shift. The lance-bombadier closed the trail and started to collect the ammu-

Top left: 'The Highway Decorators' again. The wartime caption reads: "You saw pictures of many interesting signs designed and erected by the Highland Division during their chase after Rommel. Here is their latest one in Normandy. The places named seem a long way off, there are many miles to go, but the magnificent fighting being put up by our troops will reduce these miles to journey's end and final victory."

Bottom left: Triumphant return to St Valery. Pipers of 152 Brigade, play traditional Scottish airs to the happy civilians in the main square of St Valéry-en-Caux. September 2, 1944.

Above: Troop carrying vehicles take men of 152 Brigade, across the Seine at Elbeuf. September 1944.

nition. Joe Wright appeared then, and I asked him if his retiring coy, 'D' Coy could halt and cover getting the 17 pdr away. He told them to do this, and they did without any fuss. Joe was very tired and sat down to watch the fun.

I managed to get one of my carriers into the farmyard and I was trying to get it back against the gun, all in a confined space. The driver knew what I wanted and said he could not tow away the gun. He did not tell me why, so I thought he considered the gun too heavy and so I said we would try and the men trying to move the gun out of its trench could push. He never told me that there was no hook on the back of this particular carrier to which the gun could have been attached. If he had, we would have tried to contrive something. So I stood in front of him, waving my hands about like one does directing a car into a narrow garage. Then, the Germans spotted what was going on. I had shown myself on top of the bank just before for some reason, and must have drawn their attention. Down came several "moaning minnie" bombs. A sergeant was killed outright and part of the middle joint of my right forefinger was cut off and a big piece of shrapnel went into my left thigh. All my confidence

vanished and I whimpered and ran to the other side of the carrier. I pulled myself more or less together and Bill Johnstone made me understand that there was no hook on the carrier and if we stayed any longer, we would all be hurt. He ordered the ammunition to be put on the carrier, and I managed to thank the men for their efforts and told them to go back. I was then put on top of the carrier and, with Bill holding me, we set off along the sunken lane. I was cleary visible to the Germans lying on the carrier but they did not shoot. The Wehrmacht were usually very correct in these matters, though I believe the SS types were less so.

I was taken back through the RAP, and the various RAMC stages of evacuation. At the Casualty Clearing Station, my finger was cut off, or most of it, and I received penicillin, which was something pretty new then. I was given it every two or three hours for the next few days by jabs in my lower dorsal curve, so I had very little sleep. Two days later, I was put into a Jersey-Southampton ferry boat at the Mulberry Harbour, and sailed to

Southampton in the saloon which was full of beds. We arrived at Southampton and were laid out in rows in the Customs shed before being taken by train to Ascot, and loaded into ambulance cars from 17 Canadian General Hospital at Crowthorne."

Goch (February 1945 – Battle of Rhineland)

"The object was to capture the smaller part of Goch on the south side of the River Niers. Before this, the 5th Seaforths, (Caithness and Sutherland Battalion) including Hector Mackenzie and his 'A' Company, were to capture an anti-tank ditch and, it was hoped, a bridge over a small stream and a German pill box beyond it. We, 'D' Coy, that is, were to capture the first houses in Goch, and the rest of the Fifth Battalion and then the 5/7 Gordons were to pass through into the town. The 15th and 52nd Divisions were to capture the rest of Goch on the other side of the river. At one stage, a secret weapon was to be fired at Goch and we were advised not to be forward of a certain place at the time. It was a flying mattress and it made quite a noise, but what harm it did I never saw.

Having received my orders, I went back to 'D' Coy to brief them all and give my own orders. In fact, owing to lack of time the two merged into one. The men had been well fed. Hector Mackenzie and his Seaforths had gone off to carry out their attack, and so 'D' Coy had been able to relax in the farm buildings, and were now far more awake and alert than me. This often happens in war. The officers spend most of the day buzzing about on reconnaissances, or collecting pay or dealing with one hundred little jobs, while the men hang about, resting, eating regular meals, and writing letters which the officers have to censor when they get back to the company.

The men, of course, see it differently. While the officers are having an interesting time driving all over the countryside, they have nothing to do but endless fatigues, cleaning weapons or billets. 'Gets monotonous', they say.

I did my briefing, eating my stew and pointing to the map, while the platoon commanders and Ken Buchanan pointed to theirs so everyone could see. They were all far too alert and asking bright

Refugees mingle with traffic near Goch.

questions. "Is it the 15th or 52nd Div who are moving North at 0033hrs, sir?" As if it mattered, I thought. However, the next question was a good one, and rather showed me up. "Sir, this bridge over the Niers next to the left of our objective. Oughtn't we to secure it?" 'I think we have enough to do already.' But Ian MacDonald, fresh from home and perfectly right, was not to be put off. He persisted that something had to be done about the blasted thing. But it was getting late and the Command Post was two or three miles away. A matter of this sort could hardly be discussed over the wireless or even the telephone if there was one. So I had to say it was too late to think about it now. I suppose everyone from Bill Bradford downwards had been too tired to notice this bridge on the map in the poor light and so nothing was arranged.

At the appointed time, off we went. We found Hector Mackenzie had captured the anti-tank ditch but had not pushed on to the bridge and pill box. "I thought you chaps were going to take them", he said helpfully. In fact, the bridge was not held. Indeed, we were walking over it before I realised we had come to it. A runner arrived soon after to say that his platoon commander, a much decorated sergeant from Bromley, could not find any pill boxes and was there one anyway? So we went on to our objective which was not occupied. Then, from nowhere, a German air force corporal appeared at my side, saying we had not captured his pill box and what was to become of his comrades inside it. So I told him to guide a section there and tell his pals to come out with their hands up and they would be all right. This is what happened.

The rest of the Battalion then came past and I thought we could doze for a bit, but not so. Along comes a message that we were to go on and capture the 'monastery hospital' which I luckily remembered to be a big building on our side of the main square. Goch was a market town, which I suppose was as big as Blairgowrie in my home county of Perthshire. I went forward with Pte MacInnes to see what I could do in the darkness. I reached Graham Pilcher's company, which was the forward company and, with his help, made a plan which involved sending Bill Chisholm's platoon along some back streets to my right and Sgt Delves and his platoon still further round while MacDonald stayed by Graham Pilcher in reserve. This is not perhaps exactly what I said, but it is more or less what I remember happened. Just before all this, Ian MacDonald reported that he had not only found the wretched

bridge but had crossed it and was in touch with troops on the other side, who were not interested in it any more than I had been. Luckily, Bill Bradford spoke over the wireless then, and I told him and asked if the carrier platoon, who were kept in reserve in this battle could take over so MacDonald could rejoin 'D' Coy for the next phase. This was agreed and carried out very quickly.

I sent MacInnes back for the company and Graham and I explored the cellar of the house he was in. We found a rather sticky liquor not unlike Van der Humm and some bottled gooseberries. They were unsweetened and rather nasty. Then I sat down and went to sleep. Someone woke me up, amused and rather shocked that anybody should go to sleep during a battle, and I explained my little plan. The two platoons went off, and, after a decent interval, MacInnes and I set off after them. We found Bill Chisolm and his platoon falling about in a huge bomb crater which took up the whole of a little alley they were trying to get along, but Bill was well in charge and they were pulling each other out and trying to improvise a bridge with planks from the floor of a bombed house. MacInnes and I found our way round by another street and emerged on to the main road which led from Graham Pilcher's company to the monastery hospital. It was a good wide road and that is why I had told Bill Chisholm and Sgt Delves to avoid it and go round the back streets.

There was a barricade across the street beyond the gateway into the monastery hospital and, by the gate, the German equivalent of a jeep was parked. There were some men by the barricade, and, for some reason which now escapes me, I thought they were British. I strolled over to the wee motor car, with my hands in my pockets, followed by MacInnes with the Italian Birette submachine gun he affected and which I don't think he understood, for it never worked, slung over his shoulder. I had my hands in my pockets because I found it stopped the men getting excited and so tiring themselves. If I drew my pistol, they got het up. I said: 'What have we got hold of here?' and there was a dreadful hush.

MacInnes and I appreciated the situation and decided simultaneously on the course we would follow. We turned and ran. He had a slight start, but I soon passed him and could hear the clatter of his little feet dying away behind me on the cobblestones. There were shocked cries of "Hands up Tommee" from behind the barricade and a fusillade of shots

Firing across the river into the factory area north of Goch. Sgt J Welch of Gateshead-on-Tyne.

which I noticed striking sparks from the upper parts of the houses on my left. Now, it is not very good for an officer's reputation to arrive at full speed from the direction of the enemy, followed at a respectable interval by a soldier so, as I approached Graham Pilcher's Company, I started to laugh, for the situation had its comic side and shouted "Here comes Major Brodie beating all records" or something equally ridiculous and so no-one shot at me.

Ian MacDonald's platoon were at hand and we worked our way back up the side of the street. When we got near the barricade, I took the platoon two-inch mortar into the middle of the street with one or two bombs to brass it up. The mortar man had come to me before the attack to say he had broken his glasses and was not much use without them and could he be excused. The Company was much under strength and so I had to tell him that he would have to come along carrying his mortar and someone else could shoot it off if it should be necessary. Having loaded the thing, I could not remember which way you turned the wheel which set that particular pattern off, so I had to ask. At this time the Germans were shooting, but pretty high as people usually do in the dark, so I was safe enough. He told me and I let off one or two bombs at the barricade and the firing stopped so I drew my pistol, and ran off towards the monastery hospital.

I ran through the gateway and turned right. There was a long high wall on my right with buttresses sticking out. A German was shooting at me from behind one of these and another from my left on the other side of the yard on a raised tennis court. I fired back at the German with my pistol in my left hand, and he or the one across the courtyard threw a grenade. A splinter from this hit my left shoulder blade but it only stung a bit. I ran to the next buttress and fired another couple of rounds through my revolver. Then I decided to replace the fired rounds before rushing the German in front of me. Needless to say, the ejector jammed and it was lucky the German did not rush me with his bayonet. I managed to reload and by this time both Germans had gone away.

L/Cpl Rhodes from Bill Chisholm's platoon then came up behind me with his section. His had been the first section over the bomb crater and, without waiting for the rest of his platoon, he had hurried to the sound of the firing. MacDonald's platoon were spread out in the courtyard, and various other sections had arrived from nowhere. Street fighting, like jungle fighting, presents control problems and these are made greater at night. It is really a science or skill of its own and should be carefully practised beforehand. I remembered some lectures and sand table exercises I had attended in 1943 at the Senior Officers School at, believe it or not, Poonah, and these were based on writings of heroes of the Spanish Civil war. Some of us, who had been with the Liverpool Scottish in Bambridge, County Down, had practised house to house fighting at some barracks which had been bombed,

Bringing the wounded out through a badly damaged street in Goch.

but once a battalion gets into an operation, there is no time or opportunity to practise rather specialised forms of battle, and all one can do is to bash on.

It was now getting light, and I led a party in a rush up the steps of the monastery hospital. One poor chap was shot down, but the rest of us arrived safely at the top of the stairway. We went into the porchway, and there was a glass door on the left. I threw a smoke grenade at it and it bounced back and burst a foot or two from me, so I was quite badly burned on each hand and in the face. Luckily it was not a 36 grenade, but that might have broken the glass of the door. I was in some pain and rather shaken, and had to take a pull on myself. As I did this, someone opened the door from inside and out came a young German officer with his hands up. The much decorated Sergeant from Bromley was beside me . . . trust him to get into the middle of anything exciting . . . and said "Can we have him, sir?" I asked what he meant and he pointed out that some of the younger soldiers had not killed any Germans yet. I was rather shocked, and said they could not. We were still grouped on the steps and the German officer handed me his small pistol. It was not a Lüger. I sent him off with an escort and instructions that he was to be treated decently. Then quite a number of German soldiers came out of the building and from hidey holes around the courtyard with their hands up. If we had ill-treated the officer, they would have surely fought desperately and done us some harm. I asked if any of them had been wounded by a pistol but they all said "No", which was a disappointment.

I told Ian MacDonald to consolidate the building against any counter attack while I went back to Company HQ, which was probably still with Graham Pilcher up the road. 'Yes, sir,' says Ian, 'Er, how does one consolidate a place like that?' It was not an unreasonable question, for it was a

huge building with several storeys and Ian's platoon was only about twenty strong, if that. Indeed, not the least of my reasons for going back to Company HQ was to evade this slightly awesome problem. But memories of Poonah flooded back and I gave him rather a good lecture on the subject. 'Put one or two men with grenades and bayonets at the top of any stairs leading down to the cellars and don't go into them. I'll see about a flame thrower later.' (We had noticed skylights at the bottom of the wall and, anyway, continental houses always have cellars.) 'Explore the ground floor, throwing a grenade of some sort into each room or spray it with a sten. Then dash to the far end and turn about. Don't fix bayonets because it will make the rifles too long and clumsy; if there was a hole in the ceiling, look out for bombs being dropped down. Occupy rooms facing forward and to the flanks, but don't stare straight out of the window. Hide behind the wall at the side and look out diagonally . . . Two men one on each side of the window if possible. Oh, and watch the stairs in case they rush down or roll grenades down them.'

'I see, sir,' he said 'and what about upstairs?'

'You won't have enough men for that nor for the cellars so all you can do is to cover the various stairways.' I left him to it with complete confidence. He was that sort of man.

I found that Kenneth Buchanan had brought Company HQ up the street, and we went into a house. Pte Dow's wireless, an 18 set, was working. I reported to Bill Bradford, whose custom it was to follow the leading company close enough to be in touch, but not so close as to cramp the company commander's style. He had a wireless set and operator with him and usually the Provost Sergeant and a Signals platoon motor cyclist, and, often the supporting battery commander. The artillery, though, had enormous and heavy wireless sets and this limited their ability to keep close to a thrusting commanding officer like Bill Bradford, but they did their best.

I reported that we were rather scattered and that the companies behind us must not trust us as the Germans could easily burst through us. I told him that Ian MacDonald was doing his best to consolidate the monastery hospital and would need a flame thrower to clear the cellar and I was out of touch with Sgt Delves, but Bill Chisholm and his platoon were available and I proposed to take it up the street and try to hustle the Germans away. Bill said he would push 'A' Coy (Major Taylor) through and I was to get firm. I thanked him, and said it was an excellent idea, but I was ready to push on if he would accept that the Germans might break past me.

I then rejoined Bill Chisholm in the street outside the monastery hospital. They were standing against the houses on one side of the street except for one man, who was on my side. A German machine-gun was firing down the street. It was to the credit of Bill that his men were still on the street and had not vanished into the houses where I would never have found them. I timed the bursts of machine gun fire, or rather, the intervals between them. These were about five seconds, so there was time to stroll casually across the street without haste. This I did, and the man on my side of the street followed and walked into the next burst. I was thoroughly ashamed of myself. I should have told him what to do or not to do. He is the one man for whose death I reproach myself.

The machine-gun must have gone away then, for a runner arrived from Ian Mac-Donald to say that the Germans in the cellar at the monastery hospital had sent up a white flag and would I come. I hurried along, still rather shaken, followed by Bill Chisholm and his platoon. I went into the cellar which was divided into several small rooms. I was met by an elderly German captain who told me that the colonel commanding the Goch garrison was wounded badly and wanted to surrender and would I follow him. I forget if all this was in German or English, but the rest was in German. I found the colonel lying on a stretcher on a bed with a few soldiers standing around. I saluted, and they all clicked their heels. I said that he would be well treated and could his men please carry him away. I passed the word that the men of 'D' Coy were to salute him as he was carried past, and they did. The next thing we knew was that lots of German soldiers emerged into the street from the various houses with their hands up. I suppose they saw we were civilized and would do them no harm.

I brought Company HQ and Bill Chisholm's platoon into the monastery hospital, and then a crowd of enormous tanks came rolling up the street, and in the middle, CQMS MacGregor in the jeep with a trailer and our breakfasts all hot in their hayboxes. A runner from Sgt Delves arrived and I set off with him and one or two of Company HQ carrying the breakfasts for Delves's platoon. I found them in a farmyard. On the Continent, farms are often collected together in

Above: Bren carrier dashes away after a near-miss in Goch.

Left: Field-Marshal Montgomery inspects the Guard at Div HQ. With him is Major General T G Rennie, GOC 51 Div.

villages or small towns and the farmers go out to their fields to work. In Great Britain, farm buildings are usually in the middle of the fields. Probably on the Continent, it was safer for farms to huddle together for fear of robbers.

The men of the platoon were perched up looking over the wall and out of lofts and shouting to Sgt Delves about enemy snipers trying to move about in various parts of the town. But he was too busy to bother about the enemy. 'Shoot at them', he would say. He was rather older than most of the company with a balding head and scraggy reddish moustache. He looked like a harrassed father with a lot of tiresome children and he was busy filling in a return of ammunition expended by his platoon during the night.

A little later, Brigadier Harry Cumming-Bruce came from 15 Division over the river to see me. He was a Seaforth and had been ADC to Sir Harold McMichael, the High Commissioner in Palestine in 1938-9 and frequently came to see us at Talavera Barracks. He had heard I was there and had popped over to see me, but 'D' Coy were very impressed, thinking their fame had spread abroad if a Brigadier in another Division would come across to see them while a battle was still going on. Indeed it was, and the Germans fired some heavy shells into Goch at the time. One completely destroyed a small house where I was standing and another made a big hole in the street. An armoured bulldozer drove up and pushed another complete house into it so traffic could cross.

I went to see the doctor to get my wounds tied up and he took a dim view of the phosphorous burns from the smoke grenade. Bill Bradford wanted me to be sent down the line for treatment. He afterwards told me I was rather a worry to him because he did not know how far to trust my reports, though, he agreed, they were in fact quite accurate. But I begged to stay and I was allowed to.

Later that morning, a bunch of newspapermen came to see us. One of them introduced himself as 'R. W. Thompson' which struck me as odd. Indians sometimes introduce themselves and each other using initials; 'This is Mr R. K. V. Dutt' – but I had never known a white man do this. They were all very serious and in some awe of us I thought. Mr Thompson mentioned this little meeting in a book called, as far as I remember, 'Men Under Fire'. He had a reputation, though I did not then know about it, for courage and sympathy with the front line troops. Rather earlier, a jeep load of young RAF pilots drove up to try and buy Lüger pistols. I do not think we had any at that moment, but I offered to take them forward to see, but they declined. They had enough dangers to face in their own line of business.

Since breakfast, various companies had passed through us and so had one of the Gordon battalions. The other had carried out an attack on a farm in the country nearby called Thomashof. They had had several officers killed and wounded. These men had not been to Poonah, nor read about street and house fighting in the Spanish civil war, so, when they captured the farm buildings, they did not take the precautions I told Ian MacDonald to take. The Germans had come up from the cellars and killed many of them. The Fifth Battalion was to go and sort things out and to capture an outlying cottage from which we could shoot up the main road from Goch.

The rest of the Battalion was to capture Thomashof farm and then 'D' Coy was to go off and capture the outlying cottage. The operation was, of course, handicapped by the presence of various stout-hearted Gordons hanging on in some of the buildings with no idea where the Germans or their friends were. However, the Battalion managed to occupy the farm. I arrived a little later, ahead of 'D' Coy and found that a small German patrol was loose in the farmyard and building and was entertained by the sight of Battalion HQ standing to with deadly weapons poking out in all directions. Mowat Philips, the Pioneer Officer, a little chap with a great Sten on the prowl was a particularly awesome sight. The Germans managed to break into a shed and killed a young chap in the Intelligence Section. He was a German Jew whose parents had brought him to Great Britain in about 1935. There was quite a few such, and they were good young soldiers.

Eventually, a section of another company ran into them. The Section commander bayonetted the German officer in command, who shot him in the jaw with a pistol. I do not know any more details but that was the story I heard.

'D' Coy arrived about then and we blundered off in what I hoped was the right direction. We came to Sandy Leslie and his company and he pointed out the track along which we had to go. What we had to do was go along this track for about three-quarters of a mile and then turn right across country. It was very cold and I set off at a brisk pace at the head of the company. Of course, they were smaller than me and had more to carry, so when we arrived at where we were to turn off, I found all I had were my two runners and Bill Chisholm's platoon. Then a light machine gun started firing quite close, heaven knows what at.

Having no ear for music, I asked if it sounded like a British or German machine gun, but no-one knew. Bill brightly suggested that we contact them, though he did not say how. I decided the best thing to do was to ignore it and carry out our mission. So we turned right in extended line and I put myself in front of the company and off we went. We had no supporting fire as it was hoped that we would surprise any Germans who might be in the cottage; so silence was necessary. I was still cold, and, why can't I learn? I walked briskly.

Glancing over my shoulder, I saw I was rather far in front, so I stopped and, Heaven forgive them, they stopped too. I could not shout and gestures in the dark cannot be seen, so off I went again, and they followed. Presently the cottage came in sight with some figures standing beside it. A wind was blowing in my ears but I heard a plaintive voice say 'Aber gib doch ein Antwort!'. I expect they were worried about the patrol I described just now. So, I said *Ich bin der Otto'* with my best Bavarian accent which no Bavarian recognises, and let fly with my pistol. I ran on and the platoon behind me dashed up.

Some got entangled in rose bushes but the rest joined me and the Germans all surrendered except one man in the house who threw a grenade from a window upstairs. A bit of it lodged in my throat which tickled a bit but did not hurt much. It was not too deep. Then two or three Germans came out of the house with their hands up. I asked which of them had thrown the grenade, being rather impressed really, but, naturally they did not tell me. So I sent them off with an escort.

Now, one thing which shows what a good company 'D' was. This escort had quite a long way to go and could honourably have stayed at the Command Post or taken the prisoners even further back and spent the rest of the night resting comfortably out of the battle. But not a bit of it. Shortly after, he came trotting back and said he had dumped the prisoners with the RSM and come back before he could be told to take them further. He wondered how the RSM would compete.

But meanwhile some firing broke out from in front and so I led a section forward shouting and shooting from the hip for a couple of hundred yards after telling Bill to consolidate with the rest but not to go into the house until daylight. Having chased or frightened away any Germans who might have been on our immediate front, we came back to the cottage and found that the rest of the Company under Ken Buchanan had arrived and Sergeant Delves's platoon had searched the cottage, cellar and all, a thing I would never have dared to do. Then the Germans started to mortar the place and a few of us were hit. The CSM was quite badly hit and I sent him back.

My servant, Pte Penney, said that he had been hit and could he go sick? I was hit in the leg and one or two other places, I rather forget exactly where, but nothing serious. However, being hit does sting a lot at the time and is rather a shock and what with the bitter cold – I had been sweating and the sweat seemed to be freezing on me – I was getting a bit delirious and shouting at soldiers who were only doing their job. Kenneth Buchanan and Ian MacDonald and Bill Chisholm and Sgt Delves, now acting as CSM, and the sergeant from Kent were all well up to the mark, and I decided, rightly or wrongly, that I was no longer able to inspire and might only scare everyone. So I decided to go back.

The stretcher bearers had established a small aid post in the potting shed where they had a candle and one offered to go with me. But I told him to stay and walked away. As I was going across the field a shell came over and I fell down and was hit a nasty one on one foot where the toes join the foot. My hobnails saved me, but the bone was slightly cracked. I arrived at Command Post, a pretty bloody sight, looking worse than I was. Everyone was far more sympathetic than I deserved and I reported the situation of 'D' Coy in detail. The commanding officer then put me in his jeep and sent me to RAP. On the way the jeep skidded into a ditch full of icy water, which probably did my foot good. I arrived at RAP and eventually sometime later at the Queen Elizabeth Hospital at Birmingham.

After I left, a self-propelled anti-tank gun arrived at 'D' Coy and broke down beside the cottage. However, its gun worked and it effectively stopped the Germans using the road 300yds in front all next day. Later, a German half track drove up and Ian MacDonald made a mess of it with a PIAT. Ian was mentioned in despatches and Sergeant Delves received promotion to CSM and the DCM. But, sadly, both were killed before they knew.

Bill Johnstone from 'A' Coy took over 'D' Coy. The officers were not nice to him at first and wrote to tell me he was too hard on them. Of course, he was rightly correcting the easy-going habits that had come in during my brief regime and I wrote Kenneth a fairly stiff letter, pointing out what a lot I owed to Bill Johnstone from my days in Normandy. This may have helped for by the time I rejoined at Delmanhorst near Bremen, 'D' Coy was as happy and good, perhaps better than it ever was.

I took over SP Coy again and at Bremerwurde the day before the Germans surrendered, I was accidentally shot through the arm by the Sten gun slung on a motor cyclist's back. I was sitting on the pillion and, when he kicked the starter, the thing went off. I had my hand on his shoulder and the bullet went through my arm. It hurt like hell."

One day in 1944

Soldier of the 5/7th Gordon Highlanders taking part in the fighting in the Reichswald Forest. February 1945.

Pte Ian E. Kaye (5th Bn The Black Watch) remembers:

The Battalion objective was to clear the village of Hörst in Holland. It was to be a battalion attack with 'B' Company leading and the troops to move-up in 'aircraft formation' i.e. – with alternate sections on each side of the road. The searchlight batteries in the rear would shine their lights up on to the cloud base above us and the reflecting light would provide us with an eerie half-light which was known as 'Monty's moonlight' and in which it was possible to gain a fair idea of who was friend or foe.

My company was 'B' Company and we had just enjoyed two days out of action as successive battalions of the Division passed through our positions in the leap-frogging pattern which, by now, had become familiar to us all. It was just the

job to be able to take off your boots for once and have an uninterrupted night's sleep. On the second day we spent the time writing letters home or cleaning weapons, sorting-out ammunition. Some of the Jocks had to do various chores for the Colour Sergeant. There had been the odd parade – for weapon inspection and to get our kit made-up again after items had been lost. A popular parade was the issue of cigarettes and chocolate from NAAFI supplies. The remainder of the time you either slept or talked, mostly about women and what things must be like back home. We just lived for the day and no-one thought very hard about tomorrow.

The word ran round the Company lines, 'There's an 'O' Group, and its a CO's'. We all watched carefully, as the Company Commander and his 2i/c went off to Battalion HQ that afternoon. When he came back it was his turn to hold a Company 'O' Group, where he passed-on whatever orders the commanding officer had given to him and the other company commanders. Speculation was rife as the Jocks sat waiting for the outcome, for we knew that there were many many battles ahead of us and each day we were out of the line was a bonus indeed. But we all knew, somehow, when there was to be an action and it was usually confirmed by the sight of the company runner, who wore his steel helmet if there was to be trouble. If he wore his tam 'o shanter, it was to be a cushy move instead.

This particular afternoon he wore his steel helmet, so we automatically started to get our kit sorted-out, in readiness. Soon, the platoon officer and our sergeant arrived and we were given the briefing on what was to take place. Weapons were again checked, grenades and ammunition inspected, and haversack rations issued. Section commanders were busy, looking over their men and making sure that each man knew exactly what part he was to play in the coming battle. Eventually, we were piled into trucks, and taken up to the 'Start Line', which was in the leading battalion's forward positions. We had to share their battalion lines for some hours, until the word was given to move-on.

We lay there in the darkened fields, each man thinking his own private thoughts. Personally, I always prayed to myself. I asked especially, for courage, *not* for vain glory, but merely that I might be strong enough to cope with any situation in which I might find myself, and that if I had to die, it might be quickly, please. At around three o'clock in the morning (October 29) we got the word to move. Wearily, we hauled ourselves on to our

feet in the cold damp air and listened to the whispered directions.

'We are moving straight up the road, and into the main street of the village', the Platoon Officer told us. 'The local Oranje, (Resistance fighters) have told us that Jerry isn't expecting us, and that there is very little movement of German troops. Remember, aircraft formation with Corporal Neil's section leading. If we are fired-on, that section will return the fire, and become fire section while we put in an attack with the other two. OK? If we manage to get into the village, without a fight, we move in to clear the houses, on each side of the road, and once that is done, we dig-in like billy-ho! *Right?* Let's go then, lads. Good luck, and bloody good hunting!'' (That was how he approached things. But he was a damned good bloke, and made *you* feel good too.)

So, the section started walking quietly up the road. Our corporal, with his Sten cocked at the ready, led us with great confidence. I marched at the rear, with my Bren-gun slung over my shoulder, and my finger on the trigger, and my Number 2, Private Firth, behind me, with the bag of extra magazines. Everyone's nerves were stretched like piano wires as we moved-on, and I could hear the breathing of the men near to me. I also remember feeling a bit anxious about the fact that Firth's bayonet was just inches from my behind. The major strode confidently, in the centre of the road, wearing his tam o'shanter with Red Hackle and carrying a pistol in one hand and his walking stick in the other. He had an air about him that made you feel ashamed of being scared. He whispered words of encouragement to

Top left: Lt General O'Connor seen chatting to Major Angus Ferguson, Camerons, of the Division during a parade of the massed pipe bands at Helmond in Holland, October 1944.

Bottom left: The advance on Schijndel near 's-Hertogenbosch. Jocks of the 2nd Bn Seaforths riding in Kangaroos driven by Canadians.

Above: Before crossing the Dommel canal, Scottish infantry have some food while sitting in their boats. October 24, 1944.

129

us all. 'Remember you're Black Watch and give the bastards a tanking'.

And so, 'B' Company moved steadily on, along the dim road to Hörst, with the other companies strung-out behind us. Through the uneasy dusk of the searchlights' reflection, we gradually made-out the shapes of houses, fences and gardens. But still, everything was deathly quiet, with not a thing moving, except us. My own ears seem to swivel like radar screens as I waited for the first shots to ring out. But still nothing came, and we halted, melting slowly into the darkness of the garden fences with their friendly bushes. There was the noise of an engine and slowly a jeep came along the street, with the colonel sitting on the bonnet, pistol in hand. It moved quietly until it was in line with us and the CO jumped off. He had a few words with our major, who then told us to move into the gardens, and dig-in taking care to make sure that the houses were clear first.

Our section finally dug in, working like moles in the darkness, with one man digging while the other sat with weapon at the ready, in case the Germans should be around. We had checked the two houses in our particular bit and everything seemed to be all right. In the meantime the rest of our company had dug their trenches too, and the others had passed through us towards their own objectives. There was a sudden outbreak of firing, away in front of us, and we dived into our shallow slits.

I grabbed my Bren, and whipped-off the safety catch, with my finger on the trigger and the butt cuddled to my cheek. My pal, Firth, and I sat there, listening to

Top left: Infantry wait for attack near Bokstal. October 24, 1944.

Centre left: Carriers and 6-pdr guns of the 1st Gordons move up to battle positions north of Loon-op-Zand, October 29, 1944.

Bottom left: Infantrymen of the 5th Camerons move in to the attack riding on Sherman tanks outside Sprang, North of Tilburg. October 29, 1944.

Top centre: Troops of 'A' Company, 2nd Bn Seaforths on the outskirts of the village of Drunen in November, 1944.

Top right: 5th Seaforth Highlanders Pipe Band. Wartime caption reads: "Now to get those fingers thawed out after that practice in the snow. A good log fire, an open grate and you might almost be at home." Holland, January 1945.

Right: Patrols of the 5/7th Gordon Highlanders comb out the village of Kaatsheuvel, north of Tilburg. The caption written at the time says "It is interesting to note that the majority of the men of this Regiment insist on wearing the Scottish Glengarry (in fact it is a bonnet) cap in every action: they scorn the use of the steel helmet", October 30, 1944.

the firefight going-on up ahead. The others in the section were the same, sitting in their trenches, waiting for something to happen. Every shadow seemed to wear a coal-scuttle helmet and every sound carried for a long way. We could hear more firing, then the 'crump' of mortars landing in the battalion lines and somewhere, the noise of tank tracks on the move. The shadowy figure of our corporal came up behind us and halted as we challenged him quietly. He gave us the password, and then squatted down beside us.

'You two OK? Good! Porky and Jimmy are just over there, on your right, beside that tree there. Me and Tim are at the front of the house, and Platoon HQ between the two houses. Got that? 'A' Company have just had a hell of a scrap, at the top end of the village, but no casualties that I know of. There might be a counter-attack, so for God's sake, keep your eyes open. If you see anything, let fly! They're trying to infiltrate, and we could be in trouble if they get this far. See you!'

He melted into the darkness and we crouched, staring ahead at every shifting shadow. Trees moved gently in the breeze, and I felt the sweat trickle down the small of my back. Somewhere, a dog was barking, and it had a comforting sound. For a moment I thought of my own dog, back home in another world.

132

Top left: Infantry and transport of the Division move up for the attack on the Siegfried Line. February 1945.

Centre left: Men of the 5/7th Gordon Highlanders advance through the woods adjoining the Reichwald Forest during the first phase of the attack on the Siegfried Line on the German-Holland border February 1945.

Bottom left: The glow in the sky during the RAF 'softening-up' of positions on the Brouk-Nijmegan sector on the night of February 7, 1945 preceding the attack.

Above: Men of the 7th Black Watch move through the outskirts of Brouk where they had a hard fight for their first objective, February 8, 1945.

Left: Flail tanks and other armour battle their way forward on the outskirts of Brouk. February 1945.

Gradually, oh so slowly, the shadows began to fade as dawn was coming in. We had been told that we could take turns in getting a little rest and so I was sitting in the bottom of the trench, while my pal stood guard with the Bren at the ready. I was sitting with my eyes closed, almost sleeping, when a sudden thump on the shoulder roused me. I jumped up and my mate pointed to a dark mound, just in front of our position. He whispered,

'See that mound over there. I think it's a bunker and I'm sure I saw somebody moving, once or twice. I think it's Jerries.'

My hair stiffened as I grabbed the Bren and took a sight on it. Suddenly, I, too, saw a dim white face and then another, at the foot of the mound. I almost pulled the trigger, but something made me hold back. The two faces were still there, and I thought that if they were Germans they must be thinking about surrendering, since they didn't seem to be making any move towards us. So, we watched them, for a long time, until the light grew brighter.

Eventually, a voice called *'Tommy, Nederlander, Nederlander'*. But we were suspicious, and shouted to them to come out, *'Hande hoch!'* They struggled out of the tiny doorway, with their hands up, and came slowly towards us. As they came nearer we recognised that they were Dutchmen and we welcomed them as friends. The older man turned around and called out in Dutch and the rest of the family came scrambling out of the shelter. They hugged us and shook hands with us. Each of them tried to talk at once. Since we couldn't speak their language we just smiled and waved our arms about. The sergeant came around the positions, and told us that the Germans had withdrawn a few miles ahead, and that the next brigade was going to pass through, to put in another attack, so we could relax.

We both washed and shaved, having got water from the house and it felt really good just to sit in the early morning sunshine and light-up a smoke. Suddenly, birds were singing and the night strain was a million miles away. Our Dutch family had made a breakfast, of thick bacon and eggs, with dark brown bread for each of us. So I sat on guard at the Bren-gun, whilst my mate went into the house to eat. When he returned, I went over, and was treated like a lord, as the whole family stood there watching me eat, patting me on the shoulder and calling me Tommy. I was enjoying my bacon, when the smallest child pulled at my arm. *'Tommy, kom. Muff in kellar'* he said. I laughed at his chatter, and told him that

Top left: A lone German who has had enough of the fight walks through the British lines on his way to the POW cage watched by grinning troops of the Division.

Centre left: The Division enters Germany – men of 5/7th Gordon Highlanders combing the Reichswald Forest. February 9, 1945.

Bottom left: Cooking, as done by men of the 1st Black Watch in a battered farm-house on the German border. February 1945.

Left: Even tracked vehicles found the going hard and had to be dug out. February 1945.

Below: The first infantry in the Dutch town of Gennep, 13 Pl, 'C' Coy, 5th Black Watch take another house in their advance up the main street. February 1945.

the 'Muff' (German) was avec, Kaput. 'No *Muff* now!' I said, with great bravado. But he still kept on about it. So I went with him just to humour him, and the family followed, laughing too. I kicked open the cellar door, and there stood eight fully-armed Germans!

I nearly shot through ten years growth as they all raised their hands above their heads, and shouted *'Kamerad!'* in unison. They were only too happy to be POW's and out of it all and, as I marched them down to the company "cage", I guessed that they were having a laugh, too, at the shock I had received when I opened that door.

For the rest of that day we stayed in the village and went through the familiar routine of cleaning weapons etc., in readiness for the next move. The mail came up to us and then a hot meal, and we stood down. We watched, as unit after unit passed-on up the street, with great tanks and trucks covered in camouflage and bedrolls. The pipers played in the company lines and laughing children held our hands as throngs of Dutchmen and their families came to speak to us and to watch everything we did. The afternoon gradually wore-on, and dusk began to creep over the sky. The word went round, 'CO's away to Brigade HQ, so there'll likely be another move on, tomorrow. The Camerons are having it rough, farther up. Looks as if it could be a hard scrap coming-up. Och, well, here's to the next time'.

And so, 'B' Company queued-up for its evening meal, oiled-up its weapons, and 'Got its head down' for yet another night.

Right: Life for the most part was underground in Gennep. The Germans were still making the town – a key place in their water defence line – an unhealthy place to live in, and shelled it regularly. Black Watch 'C' Coy Commander, Major G A Pilcher, MC, of the Gows, Invergowrie, Nr Dundee (centre) utilises one of the German-built cellars as his HQ. With him is his 2nd in command, Captain A L Campbell of Douglas, Isle of Man (right) and 12 Pl Commander, Lt D P Smyth of Edinburgh. February 1945.

Below: Type of country and conditions encountered on the German-Holland border. February 1945.

Far right: Sniper L/Cpl P (Dusty) Miller, Black Watch. One of the first into the town.

Forced March across Germany

Sergeant-Major Fulton in conversation with Field Marshal Montgomery at Diepholz airfield in southern Germany which had been captured only two days previously. The Field Marshal was there to meet General Eisenhower and SM Fulton and the rest of the former PoWs were waiting to be evacuated by the RAF to the United Kingdom.

While the 51st Highland Division was pressing on through Europe those who had been members of the original Division, captured at St Valery, still languished in POW camps, in particular Stalag XXB. Unknown to the majority of prisoners-of-war events were rapidly turning against the Germans as on all sides they faced determined advances. In West Prussia the Russian army was making its presence felt and in Stalag XXB during December, 1944, Sgt Major James Fulton began to get the first hints that a move was imminent. CSM James Fulton (2nd Seaforth Highlanders) recalls:

"There was a wholesale evacuation of towns and villages east of the Stalag headquarters at Marienburg owing to the Russian advance. A constant stream of military personnel and civilians passed through the town, together with vehicles of every description. Because of the obvious chaotic conditions of transport I realised that the prisoners of war of the Stalag – some ten thousand in number – could only be moved by route march. I thought, perhaps, that on the other hand we might be left where we were and ultimately be relieved by the Russian Army.

However, on January 15, 1945, there was a definite state of alarm at Stalag headquarters and it was obvious from the packing-up of the various departments and the burning of documents that a move was contemplated by the administrative staff. I was not informed what orders, if any, had been received from Berlin and I felt myself awkwardly placed as I had the responsibility, in my capacity as 'Man of Confidence',* of making the necessary arrangements in the event of an evacuation, the most important of which were the feeding of the men while on the march (which involved the issuing of remaining Red Cross stocks) and the care of those who were in hospital and could not be moved in a sudden emegency.

*The person chosen by the prisoners to make representations on their behalf to the Germans and generally be responsible for liaison between the two sides.

I waited for two or three days, expecting to be summoned by the colonel of the Stalag, but nothing happened. I decided to take matters into my own hands and on January 18 warned all prisoners of war in the main camp at Willenberg to get their things together and to prepare to march at short notice. Regarding the patients in the hospital, I requested an interview with the colonel as to what arrangements were to be made for their safety and in particular what was to happen to the stock of seven thousand invalid parcels allocated to them. I was finally granted an interview on January 21.

In answer to my question, he stated: 'I have indented for, and been promised by our headquarters at Danzig, sufficient rolling-stock to move the patients and the parcels'. At the same time he informed me that prisoners of war in the areas of Deutsch-Eylau, Rosenberg and Riesenberg (amounting to a total of some 2 300) had already started marching on January 20 while those in the Marienwerder and Stuhm areas (approximately 1 500) were starting that day.

Taking the colonel's word for it that there was rolling-stock available for the sick, but fearing that it would not be made available in time, I interviewed the senior British medical officer and, after a full discussion, we both agreed that we should continue to make what preparations were necessary for the hospital patients and staff to stay where they were – in the town of Marienburg. My fears were later justified. The transport promised was never made available. The hospitals were relieved later when the Russians attacked and entered the town. One medical orderly was killed in the attack on the town.

On January 23, at 2000 hrs, I was sent for by the Läger Commandant of the main camp (Lieut Kohlmann) who ordered me to warn all British prisoners of war to be ready to march at thirty minutes' notice as from 2230 hours. At 2300 hours we were paraded in the falling snow and at 0215 hrs on January 24, after having been issued with three days' rations by the Germans and carrying a good quantity of our own Red Cross food, blankets and other kit, we moved off from Läger Willenberg. Except for short halts, every two or three hours, we continued

140

marching through the night and all the next day along slippery roads. By 1700 hours we had covered a distance of thirty-three kilometres.

We were herded for the night into an open field at Spangaudirschau and ordered not to light fires. There was no issue of a hot meal nor even an issue of hot water. The men were tired, but the bitter cold – 18 degrees below zero – made sleep almost impossible. Some were so exhausted, however, a fact which I attributed to their never having been out of the main camp for over four years, that they just lay down where they were and fell asleep. Realising that there was a danger of them freezing to death, I ordered some of the senior NCO's to move about and wake-up those who they thought might be in danger of succumbing. It was in this way that the life of Pte Ross of the 9th HLI was saved. He had fallen asleep and when awakened, hot tea, from an unauthorised fire, was forced down his throat. After a time he revived, but he had experienced a nasty shock.

Before starting the march the next day I was besieged with requests to suggest to the officer-in-charge of the column, Lieutenant Birks, that we should march through the night and be permitted to rest during the warmest part of the day. On putting this proposal to him, the lieutenant informed me that it was the authorities' intention to provide barns for the column to sleep in during the night. This was, in fact, done during the remainder of the march, but very often these barns into which we were herded were so cold that they were no protection against the severe weather. Also, accommodation in the barns was so limited that those who arrived last at their daily destination had to sleep on straw outside, while those inside were extremely cramped for space.

On January 26 we covered twenty-six kilometres to Schridlau. Part of that journey lay across open trackless fields and was undertaken in a severe blizzard. As a result, the following morning I saw the first of the cases of frost-bite to feet and ears. As there were no doctors (British or German) with the column, attention was given to these casualties by our own medical orderlies with what meagre supplies they possessed. They worked hard against heavy odds. They attended to as many cases of frost-bite as they could, but the column was long and straggling and some parties did not get in until late at night.

Butow was reached on January 28 and 29 after a march of thirty-five kilometres through deep snow from Berent and it was here that the sick were given their first attention by a doctor. In the period of three months' marching across Germany the sick were only attended to on five occasions by a doctor. The supplies of our medical orderlies ran out early-on in the march and my repeated requests to the column officer for doctors and fresh supplies were ignored. On several occasions I had to give permission to orderlies to use razor blades to operate on men with poisoned feet.

When one soldier in the King's Own Scottish Borderers became dangerously ill I pleaded time and again with the officer to have the lad left behind in a barn along with a medical orderly so that they could be taken into the care of the advancing Russians. My requests were refused and the soldier died. When another man was shot and severely wounded by a guard I asked that he be conveyed to hospital by car. This was refused and he lay from the afternoon of February 5 in great pain in a horse-stall until admitted to hospital at mid-day on February 6 after a jolting journey of five hours in a farm cart.

Carts were ultimately placed at the disposal of the sick but the Germans had their own ideas of who was 'sick' – only those who had visible and obvious indications of their condition (large sores on the feet etc). All those suffering from dysentery and diarrhoea, a very common complaint, were curtly dealt with and left to drag themselves along as best they could with the help of a rifle-butt frequently administered. A number of men died in these tragic circumstances.

On reaching Berent on January 27, the column waited over three hours in the falling snow while billets were found. Here, the first issue of hot water since the beginning of the march was made. Even so, it was only obtained by begging and by trading some precious article such as soap.

It was at Butow that permission was given to light fires and those of us who still possessed some Red Cross food were able to make up some sort of hot meal instead of doing what we had been forced to do before – eat the frozen contents of our tins.

On January 30, again in bad weather, we covered thirty-one kilometres to Reinwasser where we were given our first hot meal since leaving Willenberg during the early hours of the morning of January 24. This 'meal' consisted of hot ersatz coffee and three or four potatoes. During actual marching days this was generally our daily fare although there were days when we received nothing at all. Sometimes I would manage to buy a horse although when this was cooked and apportioned among hundreds of men it did very little to satisfy their hunger. I spent over 500 marks for horse-meat and potatoes, being given a promise that the money would be re-imbursed. This promise was never carried out.

On February 16 we came to our first long halt – at Hasseldorf – where we stayed until February 23. This was no generous gesture on the part of the Germans. Something had gone wrong with their plans. However, the men, dangerously weak from lack of proper food, were glad of the rest. It also enabled them to get cleaned up a bit. Throughout the entire march the Germans did absolutely nothing regarding sanitary arrangements. Time and again men were turned back when seeking even some cold water to wash their faces. As they could never take off their clothes owing to the extreme severity of the weather it was inevitable that as the weeks went past lice should make their appearance. This constant body irritation, combined with malnutrition, reduced to an alarming degree the general level of their health.

Latrines were non-existent. It was sometimes prohibited to leave the barns into which the men were herded for the night. Sometimes, permission was granted for us to dig shallow trenches just outside. Then again, we were forbidden to go out after a certain hour under threat of being shot. With dysentery and diarrhoea so rife this sort of situation was responsible for the most bitter friction between the men and their guards and culminated in incidents which just fell short of being converted into shooting tragedies.

At Hasseldorf the column was split up into parties and housed in various draughty barns. These barns were in complete darkness from about five o'clock onwards in the evening and the men just had to lie down, try to sleep and wait for the dawn. During the day, rations were augmented by the purchase of vegetables from the farmers. It was found, however, that a diet of soup, the main ingredient of which was potatoes, and nothing but soup, did more harm than good in the long run.

Since the start of the march I had been trying to make what contacts I could in the search for Red Cross food, but although there were plenty of rumours as to where it was supposed to be, and I kept on petitioning the officer to allow me to verify these statements, he would not agree to my leaving the column. Eventually, on March 12 I was given permission to proceed to a place called Haggenow to collect Red Cross parcels. While on my journey there, I noticed a signpost at a village house indicating the presence of Stalag XXB headquarters. On my return to the column I requested the officer's permission to go the next day to the headquarters or, alternatively, to be visited by one of the HQ officers. Permission to go the headquarters was granted and I was escorted there on March 14 and interviewed by the colonel of the Stalag.

He opened the conversation by saying how sorry he was to learn of the hardships we had suffered. I then inquired as to the fate of the patients and staff of our hospital in Marienburg and of the personnel in some of our big camps in the Danzig, Dirschau and Berent areas. He produced his diary and showed me entries where from January 18 to 23 he had indented on five occasions for transport and that at 22.30 hours on the 23rd he had been informed that the hospital personnel would not be moved.

He said, however, that the other camps on the west of the River Vistula had started marching on February 20. I then said that as we had been marching for over fifty days under the most primitive conditions, with ever-increasing weakness, and exposed to the most inclement weather of the year, could not something possibly be done for the 9000 British prisoners of war in regard to the following points:

(1) Making an increase in the food rations.
(2) Providing proper supplies and hospital treatment for the sick.
(3) Exchanging clothing and boots. (Some men were marching with cloths tied around their feet).
(4) The supplying of a Field Service Card to each POW to allay the anxiety of his next-of-kin as the last mail received had been dated November 19, 1944.

I then asked him, would he give me information as to how many deaths had occurred since the beginning of the march? He replied that he didn't know and his adjutant was ordered to have company commanders submit a return.

Finally, I asked him how much more marching would have to be done. He said that he was entirely in the dark in regard to this. His orders were to accompany us as far as Domitz – about fifty kilometres further on. After that he and all the rest of the staff in control of the Stalag XXB columns were to return, presumably to Marienburg. (Although I had heard by this time that the Russians were in possession there). New officers would likely take over at Domitz.

The result of my interview with the colonel was passed to as many prisoners as possible, but the news was not very cheering – the colonel had been extremely vague in his reponses to my four main points – and the uncertainty of the whole march in purpose and direction did not help their morale.

On March 18 I left the column I had been marching with and was told I was being taken to Schwerin. Instead, I landed at the village of Rastow on March 20 where I met Captain I. Rose of the RAMC and five hundred men from the Danzig area. From them I learned that their treatment had been much the same as ours, but that they had been more fortunate with weather conditions.

On March 22 the majority of the five hundred prisoners of war were put to work, although I could not understand how the Germans expected men in their poor physical condition to do any labour. Some were made to convert an old brickworks into a billet and hospital for themselves; others to clear the debris and railway line at Ludwigslust after a heavy bombing raid by the RAF. Captain Rose and I made persistent complaints over a period of three days about this, saying that the men had completed a particularly strenuous march and could not be expected to work in their weak condition and on the negligible rations which they were receiving, sufficient only to keep a man alive, if that. Our protests, however, were waved aside.

On March 26, Captain Rose and I along with ninety-three men (sixty of whom belonged to Stalag XXA), the majority suffering from malnutrition and dysentery, were issued with one day's rations and put on a train. After a three days' journey during which we were packed into goods trucks without any sort of hot drink being issued, we reached Fallingbostel, the headquarters of Stalag XIB. Two hours after reaching there I was informed that a lance-corporal had died from malnutrition. This was particularly harrowing because shortly before leaving on our journey to Fallingbostel I had attended the funerals of another two prisoners who had died in the same circumstances.

During my stay at Fallingbostel I learned that the 9 000 British prisoners of war, whom I had left behind on March 18, were being employed all along the railway line from Schwerin to Magdeburg clearing debris resulting from air raids. Not only was this work which they should not have been called upon to do, but they were in constant danger from our own bombers throughout the entire period. All my protests, however, were ignored.

On April 16 to our immense relief we were relieved by the American 7th Armoured Division and two days later I was on my way home by air to Britain. For the prisoners of war it had been a long ordeal, when often the only thing left to us had been hope. It was to be a long time before the memory of those awful months on the march, through one of the toughest winters, could start to fade."

Victory Parade

Prime Minister Churchill
watching the massed pipe band
march past. March 1945.

The war was over; the Germans had surrendered. For those who had survived it was a time to celebrate – and remember; to think back to the days when it had seemed the going might be too much, to pause for a moment to reflect on friends and comrades killed in action. In Bremerhaven on May 12, 1945 the 51st Highland Division took part in a Victory Parade. Private Ian E. Kaye was serving at Brigade Headquarters. Although he did not take part in the parade he had a grandstand view as a proud spectator.

"Each Unit in the 51st Highland Division, and all the other Units in the area found a detachment to put on parade. When you considered that all these Regiments had just been on active service, it was amazing what a show they put on that day. The turn-out and bearing of these soldiers on parade was, in every sense, immaculate, and it made me feel ally proud to be one of them.

The various quartermasters must have worked miracles, to provide new battle-dress, new Divisional signs, and other items, including kilts for the Highland regiments. The troops too, must have really worked hard to ensure that their kit was 'bulled-up' to the last degree. Uniforms were pressed with razor-edged creases, belts scrubbed snow-white, and every pair of boots glittered in the sun. Every bit of brass, on belts and cap-badges, shone like mirrors, and it was hard to realise that these men, only a few weeks before, had been crawling through mud and living in slit-trenches.

The arms drill, and the standard of marching alone, would have been worthy of the Trooping of the Colour, in peacetime on Horse Guards Parade. But, on this occasion, there were no cheering crowds of civilians to applaud them. Instead, they were marching past their own mates, who lined the streets of Bremerhaven and perched like flies on every vantage point. And how we cheered them.

The parade formed-up, away on the outskirts of the town, and the morning was sunny and perfect. We, the audience, took-up our places on the main street, just across the road from the saluting base, where General Sir Brian Horrocks, the Commander of 30 Corps was to take the salute. He was a great man, who was very popular with the troops, and who never stood on ceremony in the field. Like Slim and Wavell, he had that secret built-in talent, of being able to put a man at ease, and talk to him like one of his mates. On this happy summer morning his victorious soldiers cheered him too. He stood there,

Top left: Assembling for the Rhine Battle. Scottish soldiers near the banks of the Rhine waiting for another 'D' hour. A party of the 2nd Seaforth Highlanders. March 23, 1945.

Centre left: Seaforth Highlanders in a forward signal position on the Rhine. Pte Lincoln, of Oxford (with Bren) and Sgt McRae, Rosshire, and Pte Cavill of Somerset. March 1945.

Bottom left: A self-propelled gun of the 61st Anti-tank Regiment seen on a raft prior to crossing the Rhine. A barrage balloon winch is seen in the foreground.

Right: Men of 154 Bde getting their first meal after crossing the Rhine near Rees.

Below: Highland troops boarding boats and crossing the Rhine at dawn, March 24, 1945.

Above: General Horrocks, commander of 30 Corps, talking to field commanders of the Division in the ruined town of Rees, March 1945.

Men of the 5th Seaforth Highlanders clearing the houses in Bremervörde from snipers. May 2, 1945.

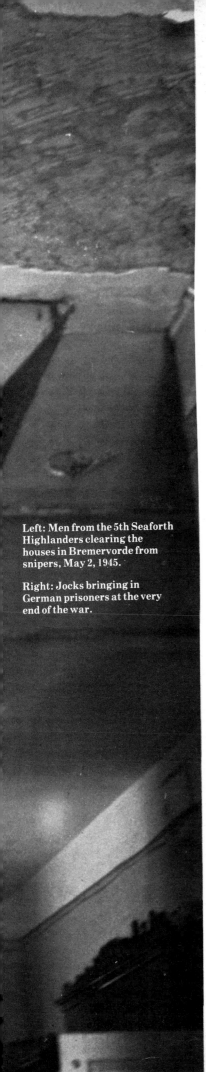

Left: Men from the 5th Seaforth Highlanders clearing the houses in Bremervorde from snipers, May 2, 1945.

Right: Jocks bringing in German prisoners at the very end of the war.

on the dais, with his staff officers around him, and he wore a big happy grin. The parade was due to start any minute, and everything suddenly went quiet as we craned our necks to look up the street for the first signs of the marching troops.

From far, far away, in the distance we heard a faint command – 'Pipes and Drums! By the left ... Quick March' and the skirling of the bagpipes could be heard all over the town. There were the combined pipe bands of all the regiments in the Highland Division, plus the Scottish Horse, who were an artillery unit. As they came into view, with kilts and sporrans swinging in unison, and the glitter of silver and brass in the sunlight, it was quite breathtaking, and a picture that will stay with me for the rest of my life; the smart drum majors, each swinging his mace with immaculate precision, and the famous 'Bearded Piper' Ashe, of the Seaforth Highlanders, who stood-out on every parade. As they marched past the General, the sound of the pipes just seemed to lift you, and we cheered our heads off.

One by one, the regiments passed us, and it was a blaze of colour, with all the different regimental tartans on display. Then came the corps troops, and the transport, followed by the big guns and

the tanks. The Middlesex Regiment, proudly wearing their HD signs on their battledress, got a special cheer from the Jocks, since they were the machine gunners in the Division, and the song of their Vickers guns was always a welcome sound to hear when we were in the Line. So, one by one, the regiments marched past their Corps Commander.

The pride he felt, was plain to see on his face. Every vehicle, tanks and trucks and guns, was shining with a new coat of paint, and every piece of rope blancoed snow white. That day, it felt good to be a British Soldier and, somehow, the war, and the long nights of strain and fear, and nights without sleep, seemed to be only a dream that we had just awakened from. It was as though it had never been.

The only thought that crossed my mind, as the parade ended, was of the many boys that we had left behind us in the long months before. But, it was, as I have said, a very splendid day, on which the streets of Bremerhaven were packed with people; but there were no Germans to be seen. They all stayed in their houses, and listened, as the victors claimed that day as their very own, and the sound of *Highland Laddie* echoed round the chimney-pots."

151

Right: German Forces surrender near Bremervörde May 5, 1945. General Raspe, Commander Corps EMS, leaving the conference held at Highland Div HQ.

Below: The occupation of Bremerhaven. Captain McMillan discussing with German officers the route to be taken into the town. Brigadier J R Sinclair, later Earl of Caithness, looks on. May 7, 1945.

Top far right: While British and German officers talk in the road, the pipes of the 7th Argylls go swinging by.

Bottom far right: Examining German firearms at the surrender of Bremerhaven.

Left: General Horrocks, GOC 30 Corps, on the saluting platform in Bremerhaven. May 1945.

Below and below right: The arrival of the massed pipe bands of HD.

Right: Troops of the Black Watch march past the saluting base under Major P S Douglas, MC. May 12, 1945.

Tributes

World War I

'Cuimhnuich gaisge agus treuntas ar sinnsear
(Remember the valour and brave deeds of our forefathers)

May 1917 –
Lieut-General (later Field Marshal Viscount) Allenby (5th Lancers), then commanding 3rd Army in France after the battle of Arras.
"Convey to 51st Division my congratulations on their great gallantry at Roeux and the Chemical Works".

Oct 1917 –
Lieut-General (later General) Sir Ivor Maxse (Coldstream Guards) then commanding 18th Corps at Passchendaele.
"The 51st Division always fights with gallantry, and can be relied on to carry out any reasonable task allotted to it in any battle. I venture to place it amongst the three best Divisions I have met in France in the last three years".

Feb 1918 –
Evening Standard Newspaper –
"The War Office has come into possession of a document of extraordinary interest. It is one recently prepared by the German HQ Staff and placed in the hands of their Divisional Commanders in the field for guidance. It is a list of British Divisions in their order of *Furchtbarkeit*, which may be translated as "much to be fearedness". In this historic list pride of place is given to the Fifty First Division.
Pall Mall Gazette – Referring to above German list: "It will be gratifying to our brothers across the Tweed that at the head of all nations and all troops is placed a certain Scottish Division.

Mar 1918 –
General Hon Julian (later Field Marshal Viscount) Byng (10th Hussars) then commanding 3rd Army in France during March Retreat, when Highland Division were transferred to 1st Army, "By their devotion and courage and splendid conduct during the stage of the great battle just completed, they have broken up overwhelming attacks and prevented the enemy gaining his object – namely a decisive victory".

1919 –
Prime Minister Lloyd George speaking of the 51st, 'Its deeds will be memorable in the history, not only of the war, but of the world.

1919 –
President Poincare of France,
"The 51st Division which has won everywhere the admiration of the Allies".

1920 –
Neil Munro LLD, the author, writing of the Highland Division,
"From the battle of Beaumont Hamel, on the Somme, in November 1916 till the fighting in October 1918, its name was on every lip, not only in the army, but at home where its exploits and reputation made it unquestionably the star performer among all infantry divisions. From every war some unit of command – a regiment or a brigade, comes through with popular laurels, a name ever after to be illustrious. In the greatest of wars that glory went to a whole division".

1924 –
Marshal of France Ferdinand Foche, Commander-in-Chief of all Allied forces in France in 1918 when unveiling the Highland Division War Memorial at Beaumont Hamel,
"I am here to render tribute to the men of the 51st Division, and most willingly I come to fulfill this duty to the men of that division, who were among the most valorous and the most sternly tried of all the troops on the Western Front".

World War II

Alba gu Brath – (Scotland for ever)

June 1940 –
Extracts from the War Diary of the German 7th Panzer Division Commander, General (later Field Marshal) Rommel referring to the 51st Highland Division
"The enemy fought desperately, first with artillery and anti-tank guns and later with machine guns and small arms. There was

particularly hard fighting round Tot and the road St Sylvian – St Valery . . . in spite of the heavy fire the British troops did not give up".

Nov 1942 –

General (later Field Marshal Viscount) Montgomery (R. Warwicks) commanding 8th Army wrote after Alamein.

"The Highland Division joined the 8th Army before the battle began. It was then untried in battle, and it had a great debt to wipe out in respect of that 'other Highland Division' which fought at St Valery in 1940.

The Highlanders went into battle in the moonlight on the night of 23rd October with the bagpipes playing, and in the fighting that followed the Highland Division gained a name for itself that will never die. The debt it owed was well and truly paid. The Division was splendidly led and fought magnificently".

Nov 1942 –

Extract from a letter sent to Commander 51st Division from General (later Lord) Freyburg, then Commander of the New Zealand Division who had the 152 Highland Brigade under his command during the "Supercharge" attack on 2nd November, at the end of the battle of Alamein.

"I cannot let your 152 Brigade go without expressing to you the admiration of my Division for the way in which the Brigade carried out its part in the operation. I was very much impressed by the training and efficiency of all ranks and everyone who came into contact with the Jocks formed the highest opinion of them".

Nov 1942 –

General (later Field Marshal Earl) Alexander (Irish Guards) then C in C Middle East, reporting to the Prime Minister on casualties after Alamein.

"Formations with most casualties are the 51st Highland Division and the 9th Australian Division, each about 2 000; 10th Armoured Division 1 350".

April 1943 –

Lt General Sir Oliver Leese Bt (Coldstream Guards) then Commander 30 Corps in a letter to Commander 51st Division after the battle of Akarit.

"I am writing to congratulate you and your Division on their magnificent fighting during the battle for the Akarit position. Your attack will be an outstanding epic in the annals of the Highland Brigade".

May 1943 –

Extract from two telegrams passing between Mr Winston Churchill, Prime Minister, to Mr Fraser, Prime Minister of New Zealand.

"General Montgomery has reported that the 30th Corps comprising the New Zealand and the 51st Highland Division is the most experienced and highly trained, and work together with unsurpassed cohesion . . ."

"The New Zealanders must enter Europe . . . In this way the association between the New Zealand Division and the 51st Highland Division – one equal temper of two heroic minds – will be preserved in the 30th Corps".

June 1943 –

Extract from a letter from General Eisenhower (US Army Commander) to Commander 51st Highland Division after an inspection, by him, of Highland Division soldiers at Algiers.

"I must say if this detachment is at all typical of your division, I can well understand why your organisation has established such an enviable record as a fighting team".

Aug 1943

General Montgomery to Commander 51st Highland Division at end of Sicilian Campaign – "Now that the campaign is over I would like to tell you how well I consider your Division has done".

Sept 1943

General Montgomery, Commander 8th Army in a letter to the recent GOC Highland Division writes of the "skilful and determined leadership of the magnificent Highland Division which played such a large part in the victories gained in Africa and in Sicily".

Aug 1944

Message from General H D J Crerar,

Commander 1st Canadian Army in France.

"Please congratulate Highland Division on fine aggressive work. The 51st of this war is showing the same unbeatable spirit which the Canadians got to know and admire in 1918".

Nov 1944

General M (later Sir Miles) Dempsey (R. Berkshires) Commander of 2nd Army to Commander 51st Highland Division in Holland.

"I want to tell you how greatly I appreciate the splendid way in which your division has fought during the recent operations. You had a great many difficulties to contend with. You overcame them all in the best possible way. Please give the Division my very sincere congratulations".

Feb 1945

Lt General (later Sir Brian) Horrocks, Commander 30th Corps to Commander 51st Highland Division.

"I have seen the 51st Highland Division fight many battles since I first met them just before Alamein. But I am certain that the Division has never fought better than in the recent offensive into Germany . . .

You have accomplished everything that you have been asked to do, in spite of the number of additional German reserves which have been thrown in on your front.

No Division has ever been asked to do more and no Division has ever accomplished more".

Mar 1945

General Dempsey again to Commander 51st Highland Division.

"Now that the battle of the Rhine has been won, and the break-out from the bridgehead is well under way, I would like to give you and your magnificent division my very sincere congratulations. Yours was one of the two* Divisions which carried out the assault crossing of the river, defeated the enemy on the other side, and paved the way for all that followed. A great achievement."

*The other Division was the 15th Scottish which consisted of Highland and Lowland Regiments.

Some post-war tributes to the Highland Division

Stainte na Gaidheil (Here's to the Highlanders)

1947

Field Marshal Viscount Alanbrooke (Royal Artillery), Chief of the Imperial General Staff in World War II.

"During the last war, I had the opportunity of seeing most of the British Divisions and Indian Divisions, many American Divisions and several French and Belgian Divisions and I can assure you that, amongst all these, the 51st unquestionably takes its place alongside the very few which, through their valour and fighting record, stand out in a category of their own".

1949

Field Marshal Viscount Montgomery of Alamein.

"Of the many fine Divisions that served under me in the Second World War, none were finer than the Highland Division. I have a very great affection for the Highland Division. It was the only Infantry Division in the armies of the British Empire that accompanied me during the whole long march from Alamein to Berlin".

1952

Lieut General Sir Brian Horrocks (Middlesex Regt) commanding 30 Corps in NW Europe – writing of Highland Division.

"Just before the Reichswald battle the Division returned to 30 Corps, its spiritual home, the offensive spirit and initiative from which it had been so renowned in North Africa were in evidence again."

1952

Field Marshal Earl Wavell (Black Watch) writing of the Highland Regiments.

"The Highland Regiments still remain the finest fighting force in the British Isles . . . The Highland Division established as great a fighting reputation as its namesake had done in the First World War."

Major Battles

Brigade Commanders

Brigade Commanders of the 51st Highland Division

Theatre of War	152 Highland Brigade		153 Highland Brigade		154 Highland Brigade		Divisional Artillery	
	Commander	Battalions	Commander	Battalions	Commander	Battalions	Commander	Units
France 1940	Brig H W V Stewart (Seaforth Highlrs)	2nd & 4th Seaforth Highlrs 4th Cameron Highlrs	Brig G T Burney (Gordon Highlrs)	4th Black Watch 1st Gordon Highlrs 5th Gordon Highlrs	Brig A C L Stanley Clark (R Scots Fusiliers)	1st Black Watch 7th A & S Highlrs 8th A & S Highlrs	Brig H C H Eden (RA)	17 Fd Regt RA 23 Fd Regt RA 75 Fd Regt RA 51st Anti-Tank Regt RA
North Africa 1942-1943	Brig G Murray (Seaforth Highlrs)	2nd & 5th Seaforth Highlrs 5th Cameron Highlrs	Brig D A H Graham (later Maj-Gen) (Cameronians)	5th Black Watch 1st Gordon Highlrs 5th/7th Gordon Highlrs	(1) Brig H W Houldsworth (later Sir Henry) (Seaforth Highlrs) (2) Brig J E Stirling (Seaforth Highlrs)	1st Black Watch 7th A & S Highlrs 7th Black Watch	Brig G M Elliot (RA)	126 Fd Regt RA 127 Fd Regt RA 128 Fd Regt RA 61 Anti-Tank Regt RA 40 Light AA Regt RA
Sicily 1943	(1) Brig G MacMillan (later Gen Sir Gordon) (A & S Highlrs) (2) Brig J A Oliver (Black Watch)	As in North Africa	Brig H Murray (later Gen Sir Horatius) (Cameron Highlrs)	As in North Africa	Brig T G Rennie (later Maj-General) (Black Watch)	As in North Africa	As in North Africa	As in North Africa
North West Europe 1944/1945	(1) Brig D H Haugh (Seaforth Highlrs) (2) Brig A J H Cassels (later Field-Marshal Sir James (Seaforth Highlanders)	As in North Africa	(1) Brig H Murray (2) Brig J R Sinclair (later Earl of Caithness) (Gordon Highlrs)	As in North Africa	Brig J A Oliver (Black Watch)	As in North Africa	Brig J Shiel (RA) (Killed in action 27 April 1945)	As in North Africa

Photo Credits

The majority of the black and white photographs in this book have been provided by the Imperial War Museum with the following exceptions: page 10 (Aberdeen Journals Ltd); page 26 (The Rommel Collection – courtesy of Herr Manfred Rommel); page 32 (Charles Shears); pages 30, 31, 33, 34, 35, 36, 37 and 138 (James Fulton); pages 55 and 98 (Brigadier James Oliver).